To Lorraine
who lived it.

Preface

We were Jehovah's Witnesses for 22 years of our adult lives, until we formally resigned from the organization known as The Watch Tower Bible and Tract Society. We did this by sending in a letter of disassociation in August 1982, requesting that our names be removed from membership.

Although the act of disassociation was simple enough, the events leading up to that decision involved a great deal. We had personally witnessed many inconsistencies down through the years but had always shelved our doubts. We lived through the 1960's and the false prophecy concerning the end of the world in 1975. However, the issue that became paramount to us was the fact that Jehovah's Witnesses had surrendered their freedom of conscience to their leadership.

This was by design; the Watch Tower Society has become an authoritarian, totalitarian organization, ruled by a group of men known as the Governing Body of Jehovah's Witnesses. This small group of men, through their representatives, wields absolute control over the consciences and lives of 3.4 million Jehovah's Witnesses. This imposition of conscience affects the lives of members in areas of health (both mental and physical) as well as marriage, raising children, education, general welfare, and almost every decision-making process imaginable.

The conscience of the Governing Body is imposed and policed through a system of "judicial committees" which maintain absolute control over the congregations. Should a person fall into disfavor with the "committee," he or she is disfellowshipped

5

(excommunicated) and must be shunned by all Jehovah's Witnesses, including relatives. Should a former member speak out against the organization, a vilification campaign is started against him. For a Jehovah's Witness today, no freedom of conscience or freedom of speech is allowed.

The following lofty words formed the lead paragraph to an article entitled 'Liberty of Conscience' in the May 17, 1939, issue of *Consolation* magazine, published by The Watch Tower Bible and Tract Society:

> This nation was founded on the principle that freedom of conscience is guaranteed to all people. Every person has the right of private judgment. No man, be he judge, governor, president, member of a legislative body, school-board principal, or any other kind of factotum, has the right or authority to determine matters of judgment for another. Each individual has the right to form his own opinions, and the right to act in accordance with those principles.

This article and many others of the period were designed to strengthen the resolve of Jehovah's Witnesses as well as soften the attitude of the public and judicial system toward them. The Watch Tower Society fought religious and civil-liberty issues for a number of years and established for themselves a remarkable record as "champions of freedom of speech and worship."

How often has history shown us examples of how the persecuted have become the persecutors and the oppressed the oppressors! Such is the case with the Watch Tower organization. The Watch Tower Society claims that all other religions are false, including all Christian denominations. They exhort all persons to examine their religion. The only religion exempt from this admonition is the Jehovah's Witnesses themselves. They also believe that it is their commission to expose false religion. The November 15, 1963, *Watchtower* magazine stated:

> It is not a form of religious persecution for anyone to *say* and to *show* that another religion is false. It is

not religious persecution for an informed person to expose publicly a certain religion as being false, thus allowing persons to see the difference between false religion and true religion. But in order to make the exposure and show the wrong religions to be false, the true worshipper will have to use an authoritative means of judgement, a rule of measurement that cannot be proved faulty. To make a public exposure of false religion is certainly of more value than exposing a news report as being untrue; it is a public service instead of a religious persecution and it has to do with the eternal life and happiness of the public. Still it leaves the public free to choose.

This book, *Witnesses of Jehovah*, was written to expose the Watch Tower as a false religion, and not as a persecution or vendetta. We feel that the public should have full disclosure as to what Jehovah's Witnesses are taught and are in turn teaching the public. The public is not given full disclosure when invited to study with Jehovah's Witnesses. People are not told that they must put aside all friends and relatives who do not agree with the Watch Tower Society and that they are joining an organization which can change the rules at any time, with all members having to change without question. The public is not aware that the Society will take control of medical and educational decisions as well as other far-reaching personal matters. They are not told that freedom of religion will be removed from them, that they will not be free to leave without severe consequences.

We desire to show and to warn the body of Christ and the public at large that the religion known as The Watch Tower Society of Jehovah's Witnesses is not an innocuous Christian variation. At the same time, it is our hope that Jehovah's Witnesses themselves might read this book and become free of Watch Tower bondage. That hope will be made difficult by the fact that this book has been banned, even before it is published, by the edict of Watch Tower policy.

What we have to tell will anger former friends and many Witnesses. That is a price we are prepared to pay. Our former friends will not have anything to do with us, nor will Jehovah's Witnesses in general. But that is their loss, not ours. We have made friends with Christ and the body of believers. We pray that someday they may join us.

—Leonard and Marjorie Chretien

Contents

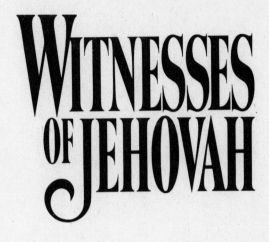

1

A History of
Disappointments

From September 30 to October 3, 1984, a unique demonstration took place in Brooklyn Heights, New York.

It is not unusual to see union members picketing their employers in order to win concessions at the bargaining table. Nor are we surprised when idealists protest a government institution or giant corporation concerning some social injustice. Even some religious activists use this method to call society's attention to gross violations of God's perceived will.

But this protest in Brooklyn was unique. It wasn't a union strike, nor a statement against government or society. Rather, 50 members and former members of a religious sect were picketing in front of the headquarters of that religious organization. The placards they waved proclaimed such unusual statements as "I Gave Up Babies," "This Religion Is a Snare and a Danger," "1884 to 1984: A Century of False Prophecy and Oppression," "Big Brother Is Watching You," "50 Years: Why Did I Leave?" and "Free After 43 Years." In front of the administration building stood a symbolic coffin. The sign on it read: "Here Lies Freedom of Conscience: Killed by the Governing Body."

One afternoon a member of that governing body boldly walked out into the midst of this crowd. As he hurried to another building one of the protestors shouted, "You are a wicked man. You'll answer to Jehovah." "Why don't you even listen to us? What are you afraid of?" yelled another. A third voice added, "You're a traitor in the name of Jesus Christ."

What organization was producing such vociferous statements?

Officially it is called the Watchtower Bible and Tract Society. Most people recognize it by the name Jehovah's Witnesses. And the protesters were more than willing to air their grievances.

Katherine Gholson was one of the picketers. She didn't go to college or plan for a career because "the end was so close. We were strongly encouraged not to get married. When I got married, we decided not to have children because we thought the end was coming in 1975."

Katherine's husband, Fred, suffered even more serious consequences from his association with the Watchtower Society. Because the organization forbids its members to participate in military service, he spent three years in prison. Ironically, it was the same penitentiary in which his father, also a Jehovah's Witness, had stayed 25 years earlier—for the exact same offense.

But a criminal record wasn't Fred's primary reason for disillusionment. As an elder he had to deal with the problems of the local congregation. He learned that even fellow elders were involved in crooked business practices and immorality. "I began to discover that we were really no better than the people outside of the organization."

Another man told of the heartrending decision he was forced to make between his religion and the life of his child. His baby boy was born with a serious hernia. An immediate operation was required to save the child's life, but that would require a blood transfusion. Jehovah's Witnesses are taught that this is against God's law, and the penalty for not obeying this rule is removal from the organization and isolation from all friends and family members who are Witnesses. The heartbroken father chose to obey "God's law," and two days later his baby died.

Others involved in the protest had experienced the pain of removal from the organization, called "disfellowshipping." Doris Toran was disfellowshipped for going to church with her husband, who is not a Jehovah's Witness. As a result, her children and grandchildren will not speak to her. "What kind of organization, going under the heading of Christian, would disallow the children and grandchildren to see their mother and grand-mother?" she asked.

These are just a few of the lives that have been scarred by the Watchtower Bible and Tract Society. We don't see this side of the picture when a Jehovah's Witness rings our doorbell or we read Watchtower propaganda. The truth hides behind an impressive array of statistics. Their daily output of printed material exceeds that of all other religious denominations combined. They brag about 3.4 million active members in 52,000 Kingdom Halls located in 208 countries and island groups around the world. And each of these members spends a minimum of ten hours a month promoting the Watchtower message and selling its literature.

What they don't tell you is the number of people who drop out of the organization, many after decades of faithful service. The membership is constantly rotating as new members come in the front door and disillusioned members go out the back door, somewhat akin to a revolving door in a department store. If Watchtower membership and baptismal statistics are analyzed over a ten-year period using their annual "Yearbook" report, an incredible shortfall is revealed. In a typical ten-year period between 750,000 and 950,000 Witnesses leave the movement. Admittedly some will have been disfellowshipped and others will have died, but a large percentage terminate their association of their own accord.

Alfred Bocksch was a Jehovah's Witness for 35 years. In the early 70's he quit his job with Ford Motor Company just four years before retirement, thereby surrendering all his benefits as an employee. He and his wife then moved to northern Michigan to gather people into the kingdom.

Why did Alfred take such a drastic step? Like all Jehovah's Witnesses at that time, he believed that Armageddon would occur in 1975, ushering in a new world order. That had been clearly taught by the Watchtower Society since the mid-1960's. Only Witnesses in good standing would survive the holocaust and enjoy the new kingdom on earth. Of course, 1975 came and went. Alfred and his wife, Marian, did some study and learned that this was the third such failed date in Watchtower's history. They did further study and began to realize that the Christ revealed in the Bible did not match the Christ taught by the Society. They finally disassociated themselves from the Society.

Alfred and Marion are by no means unique. At the demonstration in Brooklyn Heights, one picketer had left after 50 years in the organization. Another had spent 40 years, and several others more than 30. Some had been elders in their congregations. What had they learned that caused them to leave after so many years?

The Watchtower Society is a powerful organization controlling huge amounts of real estate and financial resources. They own 23 buildings in the Brooklyn Heights area alone. Marvelous old brownstones are purchased for cash, and the Society has become the largest property owners in that area of New York. It is impossible to get an accurate accounting of their assets because the Society jealously guards this information. Not even the Internal Revenue Service has access to the figures.

How has the Watchtower Society amassed such an enormous real estate and printing empire? How can they continue to expand at such a rapid rate? The Watchtower claims that this is a visible evidence of God's blessing. Yet if size and amassed wealth were a legitimate criterion, then many other religions could make that same claim. In fact, in their earlier years the Society downplayed such things, emphasizing instead the quality of the Watchtower message while criticizing Christendom's wealth and size.

The truth is that this spectacular wealth has been built on the backs of millions of sincere individuals whom the Society has turned into door-to-door salespersons of Watchtower literature. The door-to-door method of selling products from vacuum cleaners to encyclopedias has proved quite successful. However, it is not a barometer of spirituality, nor is it required to please God. Yet this is exactly how it is viewed by the average Witness. This is not by chance, but rather a clever design of the leadership. For these unpaid literature sellers are the major source of income for the Watchtower empire.

It can be demonstrated that the door-to-door ministry is highly inefficient if the goal is to attract converts. For example, statistics for 1986 indicate that it took 3014 hours of service to make one new member! That equates to one Witness working 40 hours a week for 75 weeks to make one convert. The leadership is well aware of this, yet will not consider more efficient methods. Why? Because door-to-door is the best way to sell their literature. A quick look at the money involved gives us some insight.

Witnesses believe that when they purchase their supply of literature at the local Kingdom Hall to distribute to the public, the price charged just covers the cost of printing. In actual fact, a considerable profit is made on each and every piece of literature sold. For example, the primary magazines *The Watchtower* and *Awake!* have a combined yearly sale of over 500 million copies. In a personal interview with Randall Watters, a former Watchtower headquarters staff member whose job involved printing cost analysis, we learned that during his tenure a magazine sold for 20 cents per copy, yet cost only four cents to produce. Recently the price of each magazine has been increased to 25 cents per copy. Using the same ratio, it probably costs only five cents to produce. When these magazines cross the counters at Kingdom Halls, Witnesses pay for them in cash. It is now up to the Witnesses to sell or give them away, while the Society has made an immense profit.

The Society continues to hide the huge profit margin they enjoy through the use of volunteer labor in their factories and on the doorsteps of the world. Wanting their followers to feel their work is one of ministry, they state:

> Peddling God's Word for selfish profit—how repulsive a thought! . . . Today Jehovah's Witnesses imitate the apostles' fine example in not peddling the priceless Word of God but in making it available to all.[1]

This is just one example of the credibility gap that has caused many long-standing members to abandon the Watchtower Society. It is the reason why we, the authors, have disassociated ourselves from this religion. For 22 years we were faithful Jehovah's Witnesses. For five of those years Leonard was a congregation elder. We diligently participated in door-to-door field service, conducted home Bible studies, and attended Tuesday, Thursday, and Sunday meetings. Because we were taught that only Witnesses in good standing would survive Armageddon, we even sold a prosperous business in 1972, and our home in 1974, so that we could more fully serve Jehovah in the short time before the conclusion of the present world system in 1975.

Naturally, along with many other Witnesses, we were disappointed and disillusioned when 1975 came and went. We became suspicious when the Watchtower denied responsibility for the predictions they had preached and printed during the prior decade. Instead, they laid the blame for the unfulfilled prophecy on what they called "overenthusiastic members"!

Over the next few years, we did extensive research into past Watchtower prophecies and teachings. We collected a library of old and sometimes rare copies of Watchtower literature and discovered some incredible claims made by the Society over the years. Our studies led us to conclude that the Watchtower Society is a "false prophet" organization. Deuteronomy 18:21,22, the biblical definition of a false prophet, was our criterion:

> You may say in your heart, "How shall we know the word which the Lord has not spoken?" When a prophet speaks in the name of the Lord, if the thing does not come about or come true, that is the thing which the Lord has not spoken. The prophet has spoken it presumptuously; you shall not be afraid of him.

In 1982 we sent in our letter of disassociation. With that action, a peace of mind and a freedom that we had never known in our 22 years as Jehovah's Witnesses came over us.

There are some who might think that the Watchtower Society is a harmless institution, providing a few people with a meaningful view of the Bible and life. But there are tens of thousands who know better. These are people who have suffered under the harsh demands of the organization. They have watched loved ones needlessly die because of illogical health regulations. They have given up celebrations such as Christmas and birthdays. They have surrendered higher education, careers, even marriage and children, in order to devote their lives to selling literature door-to-door. They have endured fines and imprisonment for refusing to obey certain laws of the land.

Such sacrifices might be laudable when a cause is proven truthful. But such is not the case with the Watchtower Society. Their own records condemn them. Their prophecies have not come true. Their reasonings are contradictory. Their policies are constantly changing. And their interpretations of the Bible, on which their teachings supposedly rest, frequently do not mesh with those recognized throughout history.

The purpose of this book is to reveal what we learned through our research. It is our hope that many Jehovah's Witnesses, or any who are considering joining with them, would seriously consider the evidence presented on the following pages.

Let's begin our study by examining the beginnings of the movement. To do so, we must go back in history to the mid-1800's.

2

Snake-Oil Religion

The nineteenth century was a remarkable period of change and transition for the United States. The young republic was testing and utilizing a most remarkable document—the Constitution. The nation was a beehive of activity, an experiment for the world to watch. Industrialization hastened expansion. The mighty steamboat plied the rivers while the steam locomotive pushed the nation's boundaries to the Western coastline.

Entrepreneurial activity thrived in this climate of creativity and change. The craftsman and farmer found a ready market for his goods. It was a land of promise in which immigrants by the thousands came to work and worship in peace and security. The country was open to new ideas as old traditions, ideologies, and rights were tested at every turn.

In the midst of this tumultuous setting a uniquely American character came rattling and clanging in his horse and wagon down the nation's dusty back roads. He brought his load of potions and elixirs to the villages and towns of America. His products promised cures for everything from snakebite to appendicitis. His exotic liquids and salves found a ready and open market among the populace. This unorthodox healer was the traveling medicine man or "snake-oil practitioner." There was just enough truth in his smooth pitch to attract the innocent and the naive. Many gullible persons died from putting their confidence in these untrained and uncaring healers.

During this time many persons began to doubt their religious training and faith. Darwin's theory of evolution became popular and orthodox Christianity was questioned at all levels of the population, from the intellectual to the field hand. So-called "higher criticism" took its toll as liberal theology spread throughout the country, attacking the authority of Scripture. As a result, many people found their faith destroyed.

The major American cults of today were spawned in this womb of change and upheaval. Like the snake-oil medicine men who found a ready market for their quackery, America was primed for a wave of religious quackery. The nineteenth century produced such unorthodox religious leaders as Joseph Smith, Ellen G. White, Mary Baker Eddy, Charles Taze Russell, and scores of lesser luminaries. Many of these individuals started movements that would spread from America to many parts of the world.

Charles Taze Russell, founder and President of Zion's Watch Tower Tract Society (now known as the Watch Tower Bible and Tract Society of Pennsylvania), was born on February 16, 1852, in Pittsburgh, Pennsylvania. His parents, Joseph L. and Eliza Birney Russell, were of Scottish-Irish descent and deeply religious Presbyterians. Russell's mother died when he was only nine years of age. Although she had encouraged young Russell to consider the Christian ministry, at age 11 he joined his father in business. The senior Russell owned a men's clothing store which quickly expanded to several stores under the partnership between father and son. Young Russell worked part-time in the business while completing a modest public school education, supplemented by private tutoring. At age 15 his business experience was such that he began traveling as purchasing agent for the expanding chain of stores. There is little doubt that had Russell concentrated on his entrepreneurial activities he could have gone far in the business world. Yet his early business training and experience would also serve him well for what was to come.

Adventist Renewal

As a teenager, Russell abandoned the Presbyterian Church and became a Congregationalist. His religious curiosity caused him to examine and doubt many accepted orthodox doctrines. This skepticism reached a crisis point when he was unable to defend his beliefs against an "infidel" he was trying to convert. Of this period in Russell's life *The Watchtower* says:

> The doctrine of predestination and eternal punishment gave him particular difficulty, and by the time he was seventeen he had become an avowed skeptic, discarding the Bible and the creeds of the churches.[1]

Searching for something to believe in, Russell embarked upon a study of the leading Oriental religions, but was still not satisfied. He tells what happened while he was out for a stroll one night:

> Seemingly by accident, one evening I dropped into a dusty, dingy hall in Allegheny, Pa., where I had heard that religious services were held, to see if the handful who met there had anything more sensible to offer than the creeds of the great churches. There, for the first time, I heard something of the views of Second Adventism, by Jonas Wendell, long since deceased. Thus I confess indebtedness to Adventists as well as to other Bible students.[2]

After listening to this Adventist preacher Russell's religious interest was rekindled and redirected along the adventist/millenarian theories of the time. As a mere lad of 18 he began to formulate a belief system which would be honed and adjusted throughout the rest of his life. The basic foundation would be the return of Christ and the end of the age.

Speculative Interpretation

While Christians for centuries have anticipated the return of Christ and deliverance from evil, Christ Himself warned that it is not for men to know the day or the hour. Jesus said, "Of that day and hour no one knows, not even the angels of heaven, nor the Son, but the Father alone" (Matthew 24:36). To discourage date-setting, Jesus cautioned in Mark 13:33, "Take heed, keep on the alert; for you do not know when the appointed time is." As a final warning before His ascension, our Lord stated in Acts 1:7, "It is not for you to know times or epochs which the Father has fixed by His own authority." In spite of these clear scriptural injunctions, the nineteenth century was rife with prophetic speculations, and many dates were set for the return of Christ. These ideas first circulated in Britain and continental Europe, then quickly sprang across the Atlantic to be embraced in American theological circles.[3]

This whole scheme of theology orbited around the apocalyptic books of Daniel and Revelation and the interpretation of the "seven times," "seventy weeks," 1260 days, 1290 days, and 2300 days. These end-times date-setting speculations had their origins as far back as the first century and persisted through medieval times right into the nineteenth century, where they came to full blossom. The nineteenth century saw no less than 26 expositors publishing the idea that the Gentile times of Luke 21:24 ("Jerusalem will be trampled underfoot by the Gentiles until the times of the Gentiles be fulfilled") was a period of 2520 years ending in the nineteenth or very early twentieth century, when the second advent of Christ would occur.[4]

This information was not confined to an esoteric group of individuals. It was bolstered by scores of prophetic scholars. Second-advent theology was discussed in theological journals as well as in newspapers, where information on the subject was reported as keenly as current twentieth-century explorations of space. So it was in this era that Charles Taze Russell had his interest in the second coming of Christ ignited by Second Adventist preacher Jonas Wendell.

Invisible Coming

Russell and a group of his friends and associates in Pittsburgh formed a Bible study class in which they examined theology and applied what they learned to the close of the gospel age and God's plan for mankind. They examined in detail the failed prophecies of William Miller, who had taught that the world would end in 1843 or 1844, as well as the dates of 1873 and 1874 that many Second Adventists had espoused. Not to be diverted by these failures, young Russell, then in his twenties, authored a 64-page booklet entitled *The Object and Manner of Our Lord's Return.* The publication was an interesting amalgam of concepts and ideas, some of which were common to Bible commentaries of the time.

Russell also had two Adventist mentors, George Storrs and George Stetson, and it appears that he borrowed many of his concepts from Storrs. Another mentor was Dr. Joseph A. Seiss, editor of the *Prophetic Times.* One of the ideas that Russell embraced was that Christ would be *invisibly* present before executing his wrath at Armageddon. There would be no visible coming! Benjamin Wilson of Geneva, Illinois, a member of the Church of God, authored an interlinear translation of the New Testament called the *Emphatic Diaglott.* This translation was first published in 1864, and Mr. Wilson rendered Matthew 24:3 "What will be the sign of thy presence, and of the consummation of the age?" It was claimed that the Greek word "parousia" should be properly translated "presence" rather than "coming." Russell seized upon this concept and presented the "invisible presence and two-stage coming of Christ" doctrine in his booklet. His theory was that Christ would return invisibly to choose and harvest His church. The church would be raptured and the second stage or revelation would occur at the end of the world.

An examination of Russell's eschatalogy reveals that he was an avid reader, and if not a plagiarist, certainly was given to "creative adaptation." The current leadership of the Watch Tower Bible and Tract Society likes to claim a special spiritual authority from God that they trace back to Russell. They would have the world believe that Russell uniquely understood the "times and seasons" that he found himself in, and that he was led by God to understand the element of chronology that is the backbone of their belief system to this day. Although the vast majority of millenarian groups ultimately abandoned their theories, the Watch Tower system is basically a carryover of stale nineteenth-century Adventism.

Russell needed a date to hang his theories on. In 1876 he came into possession of a copy of *The Herald of the Morning*, a magazine which indicated that the Lord's presence began in 1874 and the "harvest" had begun! The publisher was Dr. Nelson H. Barbour of Rochester, New York, a middle-aged man who had been a Millerite and was now an independent Adventist preacher. Like Russell, Barbour and his associate, John H. Paton, believed in the "invisible presence, harvest, and consummation of the age" theory, except that they had established a specific time for the events to unfold.

Young Charles Russell immediately wrote Barbour and informed him of the points they held in common respecting the purpose and manner of the Lord's return, while questioning the evidences that pointed to 1874 as being the specific year of His return. After some correspondence it was agreed that Russell would pay Barbour's expenses to meet in Philadelphia. It proved to be a most auspicious meeting. The older Barbour soon had young Russell convinced of his time-feature chronology.

Barbour had embraced the theory that the so-called "Gentile times" had begun in 606 B.C. and would end in the autumn of 1914, with Christ's kingdom fully established over the earth and the restoration of the Jews to God's favor. Russell, fired by the information gleaned from Barbour, immediately threw himself into the prophecy arena. In an autobiographical sketch Russell stated:

> I determined to curtail my business cares and give my time as well as means to the great harvest work. Accordingly, I sent Dr. Barbour back to his home, with money and instructions to prepare in concise book-form the good tidings so far as then understood,

> including the time features, while I closed out my
> Philadelphia business preparatory to engaging in the
> work, as I afterward did, traveling and preaching.
> The little book of 196 pages thus prepared was
> entitled *The Three Worlds*; and as I was enabled to give
> some time and thought to its preparation it was issued
> by us both jointly, both names appearing on its title
> page—though it was mainly written by Mr. Barbour.[5]

The book was authored by Barbour, as Russell admits. This is
not a trivial point, since essentially the chronology that Barbour
used, the so-called "times of the Gentiles," is the same that the
modern Watch Tower uses. All of its prophetic speculations are
based upon this theory. Moreover, the chronological calculation
of the "times of the Gentiles" is a basic element in the entire
doctrinal superstructure of the Watch Tower Bible and Tract
Society, including their claim to special appointment by God in
1919, a date and event which we will examine closely in Chapter 4.

The Three Worlds contained much creative adaptation, in that
Barbour's "chronology" was not entirely his own! He based the
computation of the length of the "times of the Gentiles" on the
calculations of John Aquila Brown of London, England. Brown
was the first expositor to interpret Daniel's "seven times" prophecy to Nebuchadnezzar in Daniel 4:23—"Let him share with the
beasts of the field until seven periods of time pass over him"—as
a period of 2520 years. He was also the first to apply the 2300
"year-days" of Daniel 8:14 as spanning from 457 B.C. to 1843
A.D. This had been the basis for William Miller's teaching that
the world would end in 1843 or 1844.

Of course, that date had passed, a fact which Barbour explained away by writing that the wrong thing had been expected
at the right time. So 1843/1844 retained value in the time prophecy scheme.

The Time Is at Hand

Barbour adjusted Brown's beginning of the "seven times," and the "times of the Gentiles" then became a time period of 2520 years beginning in 606 B.C. and ending in 1914 A.D. This meant that much was to happen between 1874 and 1914. It was argued that Christ had come invisibly in 1874, the harvest had begun, the saints would be raptured, and the world would experience a time of trouble and woe such as it had never seen before. All of this was to culminate in 1914, when Christ's kingdom would have full sway.

So it was that in 1877, at the age of 25, Russell adopted and adapted his eschatological system from Dr. Joseph Seiss and Dr. Nelson H. Barbour, along with concepts from a bevy of obscure writers of the time. Having assembled his "theological salad," Russell set out to inform and warn the world. To accomplish this Russell founded a new magazine, *Zion's Watch Tower and Herald of Christ's Presence*, in July 1879. Today the magazine is called *The Watchtower*. Russell used this magazine to promulgate his views that the world entered its time of the end in 1799, Christ had returned invisibly in 1874, the great harvest was in progress, the rapture was imminent, and the world would end in 1914!

This message was to be the theme and thrust of Russell's work for the next 35 years. He and his followers tirelessly spread the word, and soon congregations (called "ecclesias") were organized in several cities. They were modeled after the Pittsburgh group, of which Russell was the elected "pastor."

In 1879 Russell married Maria Frances Ackley. She was a pretty, petite woman who proved a very able and intelligent partner. Maria wrote articles for *Zion's Watch Tower* and helped answer the many letters that came in. But it was a celibate and therefore childless marriage, and it became a stormy alliance that ended in a separation in 1897. A bitter trial legalized the separation in 1906. Maria, however, served as a loyal supporter of Charles Russell during the better years of their marriage and also served as secretary-treasurer of Zion's Watch Tower Society, which was incorporated in 1884.

After deciding on his "end of the age" and "invisible presence" teachings, Russell started to develop a systematic theology which included doctrines that were unorthodox. He rejected the immortality of the human soul and the doctrine of hell. By 1882 he openly rejected the trinity. He taught that the church, or bride of Christ, was limited to 144,000 members. Most persons would gain salvation as a secondary heavenly class and would survive the end of the age to live in a paradise on earth.

The modern Witness believes that Russell was selected and used by God because of his understanding of the various facets of the return of Christ and the end of the age. The evidence proves otherwise. The doctrinal system he developed was nothing more than a rehash of concepts and beliefs derived from other people whose theories had been in existence for a long time. Probably the only unique feature about Russell was that he took all these borrowed concepts and applied smart merchandising methods to spread them far and wide. His early business experience served him well for the message he felt impelled to tell.

The Gathering Storm

Charles Taze Russell was a true delusionary, and as such he was prepared to expend both his energy and his resources for the cause. He believed that the preaching campaign would be finished by 1914 with the consummation of the age, and so devoted his funds and time to the work at hand. Russell recognized that the task of gathering the elect and warning the world was too large an undertaking for himself and his close associates, so in 1881 he put out a call for preachers.[6]

The response was tremendous. The message that the elect were being gathered and the world would end in 1914 drew hundreds of evangelists. With great enthusiasm they hit the road loaded with magazines, books, and tracts, which they sold, using part of the revenue to sustain themselves. This work was done for the most part by single persons or childless couples. Within months of the call for preachers, Russell stated that all who wanted to go to heaven should be preachers, thereby guaranteeing him a large contingent of proselytizers.[7]

To keep his zealous army supplied with material to sell to the public, Russell began to write an enormous number of articles, tracts, books, and sermons. The first of a series of books that were to become the backbone of Watch Tower theology for decades was Volume 1 of the *Millennial Dawn Series*, called *The Divine Plan of the Ages*. In this book Russell provided the first real foundation upon which all his subsequent theology would be based.[8] It was published in 1886, and the series ran to six volumes. The last one was published in 1904 when the series was renamed *Studies in the Scriptures*. After Russell's death the Society produced a seventh volume in 1917, entitled *The Finished Mystery*, which was ostensibly Russell's posthumous work.

God's Stone Witness

A new addition was incorporated into Russell's theological stew in 1881 when he extolled the Great Pyramid of Gizeh as "a miracle in stone," "not planned by men but a work of God."[9] He declared that the pyramid corroborated the Scriptures and that the measurements of the grand gallery confirmed his prophetic dates![10]

Was this a new and enlightened revelation? No. In fact, pyramidology had been in fashion for some time. John Taylor and Charles Piazzi Smyth, Astronomer Royal of Scotland, both authored popular books on the subject in the mid-1800's. Charles Russell, an avid reader and student of pseudoreligious theories, was no doubt also influenced by his mentor, Dr. Joseph A. Seiss, who outlined his pyramid concepts in a book entitled *The Great Pyramid: A Miracle in Stone*, written in 1877.

Russell devoted an entire chapter to the pyramid in the third volume (published in 1891) of *Studies in the Scriptures*. By measuring the various passageways of the Great Pyramid and then substituting the inches for years, a new twist in Russell's chronological scheme was introduced to his readers. An example of this reasoning is found on page 342 of Volume 3:

Then measuring *down* the "Entrance Passage" from that point, to find the distance to the entrance of the "Pit," representing the great trouble and destruction with which this age is to close, when evil will be overthrown from power, we find it to be 3416 inches, symbolizing 3416 years from the above date, B.C. 1542. This calculation shows A.D. 1874 as marking the beginning of the period of trouble; for 1542 years B.C. plus 1874 years A.D. equals 3416 years. Thus the Pyramid witnesses that the close of 1874 was the *chronological* beginning of the time of trouble such as was not since there was a nation—no, nor ever shall be afterward.

In later editions the Watchtower Society used an "inch-stretcher" to change the inches and therefore the date to accommodate their speculations. The 3416 inches became 3457 inches and, presto, 1874 became 1915! The changing of dates to "adjust" for their failures remains a Watch Tower tradition to this day.

The belief that the Great Pyramid was an instrument of God was central to Watch Tower doctrine and tenaciously held for almost 50 years of their history. This was enunciated quite clearly in the March 15, 1911, issue of *The Watch Tower*.

No doubt all of our readers have read Studies in the Scriptures, Vol. III, the last chapter of which describes the Pyramid and sets forth much of the wonderful symbolic teachings shown in its construction. It shows the Pyramid to be in exact harmony with the Bible. Indeed, some, after reading this volume, have referred to the Great Pyramid as "The Bible in stone."[11]

The significance of the acceptance by Russell and his followers of pyramidology has a sinister overtone to it. The Great Pyramid figures prominently in many medieval and Renaissance cults, especially in the Rosicrucian and occult traditions.[12]

To what degree was Russell influenced by the Eastern religions he studied as a teenage boy? The influence of occultic worship on Russell's theology may be stronger than most persons realize. Stamped in gold on the front covers of the *Studies in the Scriptures* series is a winged solar disk. This symbol originated in ancient Egypt, where it was the quintessential symbol representing Horus, the sun god. The winged disk was used throughout the centuries to represent the supreme god of other pagan cults and societies. It was the symbol for the Baal gods during Jezebel's reign, as well as the god of the Zoroastrian cult, founded by Zoroaster, the Persian religious prophet whom Russell wrote about with admiration.

All of this takes on even greater meaning when we consider that the Watch Tower Society makes the grandiose claim that God has been using them uniquely since their inception. Though modern-day Witnesses are no longer taught the pyramid theories, they may be surprised to learn that some of the Society's present teachings have their roots in those theories. Russell used the pyramid to corroborate the year 1914, which is the cornerstone in the Witnesses' doctrinal system.

In 1928, some 47 years after "the Bible in stone" doctrine was embraced by Russell, the second president of the Watch Tower Society, Joseph Rutherford, declared that it was *not* ordained by God. In the November 15, 1928, *Watchtower,* on page 344, Rutherford wrote:

> It is more reasonable to conclude that the Great Pyramid of Gizeh as well as the other pyramids thereabout, also the sphinx, were built by the rulers of Egypt and under the direction of Satan the Devil.

Even though pyramidology was abandoned in 1928, as late as 1944 the Watch Tower organization continued to sell the books containing this erroneous teaching.[13] At the gravesite of Charles Taze Russell in Pennsylvania stands a massive stone pyramid weighing several tons—an embarrassing reminder of his false prophetic speculations and belief system.

Faithful and Wise Servant

In Matthew 24:45 Jesus asked the disciples a rhetorical question: "Who then is a faithful and wise servant, whom his lord hath made ruler over his household, to give them meat in due season?" (KJV). Jesus posed this question to remind His disciples to be faithful and diligent in their duties as servants of Christ.

During the years 1879 to 1895 Russell held the view that the "servant" was the 144,000-member Church. Although his authority was being questioned by some prominent Bible Students (as Jehovah's Witnesses were called until 1931), the concept of a singular "servant" was nevertheless beginning to germinate. It came to fruition in 1894, when some prominent members defected from Russell's movement over the issue of Russell's authority. In an attempt to defend her husband from their accusations, Maria Russell reinforced the idea that C.T. Russell was indeed "that servant." Russell embraced his wife's flattering doctrine and used his magazine to print letters from his followers extolling him as "that servant." Within a short time, most of the Bible Students accepted the idea that Russell was God's special spokesman, His "channel" dispensing spiritual food to the Church. However, the press and public weren't convinced; they derisively called his followers Russellites.

One year after his death, the Watch Tower Society wrote concerning the special position: "In 1878 the stewardship of the things of God, the teaching of Bible truths, was taken from the clergy, unfaithful to their age-long stewardship, and given to Pastor Russell. . . . Then in 1881, he became God's watchman for all Christendom, and began his gigantic work of witness."[14] It was further stated that Russell was "the greatest servant whom the Church of God has had since the Apostle Paul." He was listed along with the apostles Paul and John, and Arius, Waldo, Wycliffe, and Luther, with Russell being the seventh "messenger" to the Church![15]

As if this were not enough to convince the world of Russell's divine ordination and work, *The Finished Mystery* spells it out:

In all his warnings he claimed no originality. He said that he could never have written his books himself. It all came from God, through the enlightenment of the Holy Spirit.[16]

The Bible Rearranged

What the Bible Students were taught by Russell was extra-biblical and was promulgated as being on a level as high as or higher than the Bible itself. The six volumes of *Scripture Studies* were called by the Society "the Bible in an arranged form."[17] The Bible Students were reminded that Pastor Russell's *Studies* were the key to scriptural understanding, superseding even the Bible itself. Without them they would go into darkness:

> Furthermore, not only do we find that people cannot see the divine plan in studying the Bible by itself, but we see, also, that if anyone lays the *Scripture Studies* aside, even after he has used them, after he has become familiar with them, after he has read them for ten years—if he then lays them aside and ignores them and goes to the Bible alone, though he has understood his Bible for ten years, our experience shows that within two years he goes into darkness. On the other hand, if he had merely read the *Scripture Studies* with their references, and had not read a page of the Bible, as such, he would be in the light at the end of the two years, because he would have the light of the Scriptures.[18]

Sad to say, 70 years after the death of Russell there are thousands of persons who still view these writings with that same high regard! Although the modern Watch Tower has abandoned the more fanciful interpretations and speculations of the *Studies in the Scriptures*, quite a number of breakaway groups are still basically Russellite in belief and structure.

The End Is Nigh

By 1908 the Society had outgrown its facilities in Pittsburgh and had decided to move its headquarters to Brooklyn, New York, which was better suited for worldwide shipping and communication. They purchased the old "Plymouth Bethel" on Hicks Street and renamed it "The Brooklyn Tabernacle." It had a second-floor auditorium seating 800. The street floor was remodeled to be the Society's operating office while the large basement housed a small printery as well as a stock and shipping department. An old home on nearby Columbia Heights was also purchased to house more than 30 full-time members of the headquarters staff. Three years later a spacious new dormitory was added. All this was an embryonic prelude to what has become a virtual takeover of the historic Brooklyn Heights area.

The Bible Students suffered many prophetic disappointments as a result of Russell's teaching. However, the greatest disappointment by far was his speculation concerning the end of the world in 1914 (when it was predicted that his followers would be raptured and the Kingdom of God would be established). The information that the Bible Students received direct from "God's mouthpiece" constantly reminded them of the nearness of "the battle of the great day of God Almighty" and the end of the world. This was purported to be not just guesswork on Russell's part but a fact definitely indicated by Scripture. On January 15, 1892, Russell wrote:

> The date of the close of that "battle" is definitely marked in Scripture as October, 1914. It is already in progress, its beginning dating from October, 1874.[19]

Russellites were admonished that the setting up of God's Kingdom had begun and that the current world order was almost over. According to Volume II of *Studies in the Scriptures*, 1889:

> Be not surprised, then, when in subsequent chapters we present proofs that the setting up of the Kingdom of God is already begun, that it is pointed out in

prophecy as due to begin the exercise of power in A.D. 1878, and that the "battle of the great day of God Almighty" (Rev. 16:14), which will end in A.D. 1914 with the complete overthrow of earth's present rulership, is already commenced.[20]

Russell's hatred of the churches and clergy manifested itself in his prophecy framework. Christendom was put on notice that her end was near:

> . . . the Gospel age harvest will end October, 1914, and that likewise the overthrow of "Christendom," so-called, must be expected to immediately follow. "In one hour" judgment shall come upon her.[21]

Some of the readers of Watch Tower publications wrote in to see if there was any possibility of a mistake in the calculations. They were reassured by the following statement in *Zion's Watch Tower* of July 15, 1894:

> We see no reason for changing the figures—nor could we change them if we would. They are, we believe, God's dates, not ours. But bear in mind that the end of 1914 is not the date for the *beginning*, but for the *end* of the time of trouble.

Shell Game

Today the Watch Tower Society glosses over these predictions. They point to some of the cautionary statements that Russell finally began to use as 1914 drew near. In later editions of the *Studies in the Scriptures* the dates were manipulated and changed. Like clay, the facts were molded and shaped to fit the moment.

In a rare admission, the second president of the Watch Tower Society wrote in Volume I of *Light*, published in 1930, on page 194:

All of the Lord's people looked forward to 1914 with joyful expectation. When that time came and passed there was much disappointment, chagrin and mourning, and the Lord's people were greatly in reproach. They were ridiculed by the clergy and their allies in particular, and pointed to with scorn, because they had said so much about 1914, and what would come to pass, and their "prophecies" had not been fulfilled.

It is interesting to note that many Bible Students in the era prior to 1914 sold their homes and arranged their affairs around that date. Witnesses would do the same when their leaders again predicted the end of the world for 1925 and 1975.

Russell's peculiar beliefs and endorsements would border on the humorous if it were not for the fact that people's lives were involved. He endorsed a number of quack medical treatments and promoted them in the *Watch Tower*—cures for pneumonia, grippe, typhoid, and skin cancer, all of which were nothing more than "snake-oil" or "folk" methods.[22]

Charles Taze Russell left a legacy of prophetic speculation, pseudoreligious theology, and pseudoscientific, pseudomedical quackery that persists in the present-day Watch Tower organization with continued change and adaptation (a hallmark of Watch Tower policy). His life was plagued by lawsuits, controversy, a disintegrated marriage, and the failure of all his prophecies. In his lifetime he played many roles, some of which were ascribed to him by his followers—businessman, orator, writer, teacher, Bible exegete, scholar, historian, medical advisor, and, above all, prophet of God.

On October 31, 1916, while on board a train returning from a lecture tour on the West Coast, Russell was very sick and sensed that death was near. He asked his traveling companion to fashion him a Roman toga from the bedsheets. After donning the toga he had his aide call in the Pullman conductor and the porter so that they could see "how a great man of God can die." A few days later the reverential importance that Russell held among the Bible Students was evident in a eulogy given at his funeral:

> ... like the disciples of old our own hearts burned within us as we listened to his clear and beautiful unfolding of the Word of God. We thus learned that we were sitting at the feet of God, and also the greatest Bible scholar since the days of the apostles.[23]

3

Advertise the King and His Kingdom

Following the death of Charles Taze Russell, the saga of the Watch Tower Bible and Tract Society begins to sound more like a period novel, with a protaganist the equal of Elmer Gantry or the Great Gatsby. The Roaring Twenties and the Great Depression form the backdrop for a plot full of back-stabbing intrigue, a charismatic leader living an opulent lifestyle, and a mass movement embracing tens of thousands of people looking for hope.

The key figure in this 25-year saga is Joseph Franklin Rutherford, who molded the Watch Tower Society into the highly controlled hierarchical organization that it is today. He was a tall, imposing man who looked more like a senator than most senators. His loud, commanding voice coupled with a bombastic, vaudevillian speaking style made him an overbearing personality. In 1896 he put his oratorical skills to work campaigning for William Jennings Bryan in his unsuccessful bid for the Presidency. He adopted Bryan's collar-up shirt style of dress in honor of his political hero and retained this unique clothing style until his death in 1942, decades after the fashion had been abandoned by all but the most eccentric.

Rutherford was introduced to Russell's teachings in 1894, at the age of 25, but did not actually join the movement until 1906. By then he had developed a successful legal career as a public prosecutor. On four occasions he substituted for a local judge when the judge was unable to preside, and thereafter he was always known as "Judge" Rutherford. Soon after he joined the Society, he became its legal counselor and developed a following among the Bible Students for his defense of Russell and the Society in numerous law cases. Thus the stage was set for the Judge to set himself up for election as the Society's second president following Russell's death.

The actual election was a story of tough back-room conspiracy. By incredible manipulations, Rutherford engineered the removal of four of the directors[1] and denigrated the candidacy of the strong contenders for the office.[2] With his primary opposition removed, he was elected president on January 6, 1917.

Things moved rapidly after Rutherford's election. He commissioned the printing of the seventh volume of *Studies in the Scriptures*, entitled *The Finished Mystery*. Essentially it was a verse-by-verse commentary on the books of Revelation, Ezekiel, and the Song of Solomon. It was ostensibly the posthumous work of C.T. Russell. Though utilizing some of Russell's notes, it was actually written by C.J. Woodworth and G.H. Fisher.

This was the most controversial book ever printed by the Watch Tower Society. The fantastic exegesis and fanciful explanations of biblical verses strain credulity. Rutherford released the book on July 17, 1917, at mealtime in the dining room of Watch Tower headquarters in Brooklyn. Pandemonium broke out among the staff. A seething undercurrent of dissension that had existed since Rutherford's election finally surfaced. P.S.L. Johnson, the deposed directors, and other supporters engaged Rutherford in a heated, bitter debate which lasted five hours. The exchange degenerated into a riot, with individuals shaking their fists and throwing hard rolls at Rutherford.[3]

A few days later Judge Rutherford ordered the deposed directors to leave the Bethel home. The police were summoned to eject them from the Society's offices. These events set the tone for Rutherford's presidency, and resulted in a serious division. Watch Tower statistics indicate a loss of approximately 20 percent of their membership when a number of breakaway movements began at this time.

Ironically, it was the United States government that stopped the exit and solidified the Judge's power. The country was deeply embroiled in World War I and patriotism was running high when the Society launched an insulting and stinging campaign against the clergy's support of the war. *The Finished Mystery* and other literature contained virulent attacks on the clergy (whom Rutherford labeled "the Swine Class") and military service. As a result, Judge Rutherford and seven directors of the Watch Tower Society were arrested and charged with sedition. Rutherford and six of the directors were sentenced to 20 years each and one director to ten years in the Federal Penitentiary at Atlanta, Georgia. As it turned out, the Judge and his fellow directors were released on bail in March, 1919, after nine months of imprisonment. A year later the United States government dropped all charges.

Rutherford came out of prison like a provoked badger, even more determined to wage war on the triumvirate of clergy, politics, and big business, whom he believed were responsible for his imprisonment. He returned to headquarters a martyr, his position consolidated within the ranks of the faithful.

To revive the somewhat moribund organization, he called a general convention at Cedar Point, Ohio, for September 1-7, 1919. It amounted to a "call to arms" for the 6000 individuals who attended. The official Watch Tower history presents this convention as earth-shattering in significance and indicates that the membership received their "marching orders" from Jehovah.[4]

Shortly thereafter a worldwide campaign was launched, centered around the slogan *Millions Now Living Will Never Die*. A booklet by that title became a big seller for the Society. In it the world was put on notice that it would be destroyed by 1925. But those who joined the Watch Tower organization would be spared. It also stated that Abraham, Isaac, Jacob, and other faithful servants of God from the pre-Christian era would be resurrected in that same year to usher in a righteous government under the auspices of the Watch Tower Society.[5]

By a convoluted exegesis of Scripture it was argued that the world sytem would end and that reconstruction would begin in 1925:

Based upon the argument heretofore set forth, then, that the old order of things, the old world, is ending and is therefore passing away, and that the new order is coming in, and that 1925 shall mark the resurrection of the faithful worthies of old and the beginning of reconstruction, it is reasonable to conclude that millions of people now on the earth will be still on the earth in 1925. Then, based upon the promises set forth in the divine Word, we must reach the positive and indisputable conclusion that millions now living will never die.[6]

Merchandising Kickoff

The message was electrifying and timely to people of the early 1920's. The world had just agonized through the first Great War that had taken the lives of millions and destroyed entire cities. Multitudes suffered from food shortages and millions died from the Spanish influenza epidemic near the conclusion of the war. People were ready to latch onto a message of hope.

The impetus from this message was accelerated by a full-scale sales promotion effort. The Judge envisaged a worldwide organization that would eclipse anything accomplished by Russell. In order to raise the large amounts of money he needed, Rutherford fixed upon the idea of a vast advertising campaign to sell literature published by the Watch Tower Society. This would be accomplished by having volunteers peddle these wares door-to-door. The kickoff was the September, 1922, Cedar Point Convention.

Rutherford delivered the keynote talk, entitled "The Kingdom," hyping the audience with the responsibility which they held to warn the world of its impending destruction in 1925. He wound up the speech by declaring:

Do you believe it! Do you believe that the King of glory is present, and has been since 1874? . . . Behold,

the King reigns! you are his publicity agents. Therefore advertise, advertise, advertise, the King and his
kingdom.[7]

With this statement a large 36-foot banner was unfurled above
Rutherford's head. It read: ADVERTISE THE KING AND
KINGDOM.[8] The response was positive, and the energetic work
began immediately.

This convention proved to be a successful sales promotion
extravaganza for the Watch Tower organization. The movement
gained the momentum of a freight train. Handbills, newspaper
ads, posters, huge billboards, and radio broadcasts heralded the
message that "millions now living will never die."

But the tireless door-to-door worker remained the vital element in this scheme. Many Watch Tower members sold their
homes and businesses and took to the road like itinerant peddlers.
Living in cars, trucks, and trailers, they went from door to door
through village and town, spreading the word.

Two innovative full-time workers were Roy and Maud Good-
rich, who traveled throughout the southern United States. They
lived in a Model T Ford touring car, which served as their home.
They were so adept at bookselling that the Judge used them at
conventions to testify how they could live by trading books for
eggs, chickens, and other necessities. But 20 years later they
denounced the Watch Tower organization for promoting certain
quack health practices. As a reward for their desire to keep the
organization pure, they were excommunicated. They spent their
remaining years trying to expose the credibility gap in the organization.

Blame the Devil

The main teaching journal, *The Watch Tower*, continually
stressed the accuracy of the 1925 date. For example, the July 15,
1924, issue stated on page 211:

The year 1925 is a date definitely and clearly marked
in the Scriptures, even more clearly than that of 1914.

Membership's belief in this date was so total that many farmers did not plant crops in the spring of 1925! The authors were personally told of two examples of this in western Canada. In one case the Witness told us that his grandfather went ahead and planted his crops in the spring, though other members of his congregation did not. The congregation elders chastised this man for his lack of faith. That winter the grandfather was looked to for assistance by those who had not planted their crops.

However, the Judge had become a little more cautionary. The January 1, 1925, issue of the magazine stated on page 3:

> The year 1925 is here. With great expectation Christians have looked forward to this year. Many have confidently expected that all members of the body of Christ will be changed to heavenly glory during the year. This may be accomplished. It may not be. In his own due time God will accomplish his purposes concerning his own people.
>
> Christians should not be so deeply concerned about what may *transpire* during this year that they would fail to joyfully *do* what the Lord would have them to do.

Of course, the year 1925 came and went. Expectations were not fulfilled. Instead, the roaring 20's were in full swing. While the faithful continued to sell books and warn the world, many were discouraged. Membership plummeted back to 1920 levels.[9] Rutherford, in a classic buck-passing maneuver, blamed the devil for the disappointment that was growing among his followers. He stated in the September 1, 1925, *Watchtower* (page 262):

> It is to be expected that Satan will try to inject into the minds of the consecrated the thought that 1925 should see an end of the work, and that therefore it would be needless for them to do more.

Today the Watch Tower organization casually dismisses the whole 1925 debacle as the speculations of overzealous members:

So, as Anna MacDonald recalls: 1925 was a sad year for many brothers. Some of them were stumbled; their hopes were dashed. They had hoped to see some of the "ancient worthies" resurrected. Instead of its being considered a "probability," they read into it that it was a "certainty," and some prepared for their own loved ones with expectancy of their resurrection.[10]

Peddlers of Paradise

It took several years for the Society to recover from the 1925 setback and regain the momentum of the "Millions Now Living Will Never Die" campaign. The stock market crash of 1929 was a turning point.

The Society has always capitalized on every disaster, whether man-made or natural, to attract followers. The Great Depression created a vast pool of dissatisfied people. This was tailor-made for the Watch Tower Society, since it claimed that the depression was another sign of the end of the world. Many bewildered and unhappy people joined the Watch Tower Society. Since many of the newcomers were unemployed, they gravitated toward "pioneer service." Pioneers were basically full-time booksellers who received a pitiful discount on the literature which they then retailed door to door throughout America and other lands in which the Society had established a foothold.

Employing the same zeal and methods used in the "Millions" campaign, the message of the impending end of the world spread far and wide. Every conceivable avenue of proselytizing and bookselling was utilized. Many members built house trailers with blueprints supplied by the Society and then forged out into the hinterlands. Some traveled by train or bus to isolated areas. The standard of spirituality and commitment to Jehovah was measured by the number of hours spent in the field and the amount of literature sold.

Meanwhile, what was the Society's president doing to support the sacrificial efforts of the membership? In 1929 Judge Rutherford purchased a large lot in an exclusive residential district of

San Diego. On it he commissioned the building of a palatial mansion and chose one of San Diego's most notable architects, Richard Requa, to design the home.[11] The construction cost in excess of 75,000 dollars in depression dollars. That amount may not seem much by today's standards, but it was a significant amount at the time when a very nice home could be purchased for 3000 to 5000 dollars.

The mansion was completed in 1930 and the Judge wintered there until his death in 1942. He named it Beth Sarim, which in Hebrew means House of the Princes. In spite of the failure of 1925, Judge Rutherford continued to stress that the end was close and that the faithful men of old, the "Princes," could be expected at any time. Rutherford rationalized that since San Diego's climate was very similar to that of Palestine, it would be appropriate to build a house there for the soon-to-be-resurrected "Princes." Apparently the Judge thought he had some inside knowledge that the God of the universe would choose San Diego, California, as the place to resurrect these faithful men of old!

To further authenticate this idea, Rutherford drafted what is probably the most unusual property deed ever recorded in America. The property was deeded to the Watch Tower Bible and Tract Society to be held in trust for these ancient worthies. The house would be turned over to them when they appeared and properly identified themselves.[12] To make sure that everybody understood just who these representatives of God were, such individuals as David, Gideon, Barak, Samson, Jephthah, Joseph, and Samuel were named.[13] A provision in the deed allowed the Judge exclusive use of the property during his lifetime.

In order that the Princes would have transportation befitting their station, a brand-new 16-cylinder Cadillac coupe sat ready in the garage. How all the Princes were to fit in the flashy yellow coupe was never discussed. To place the value of this automobile in perspective, a new Ford in 1931 cost approximately 600 dollars. A 16-cylinder Cadillac cost between 5400 and 9200 dollars, depending on style. Another V-16 Cadillac convertible sedan was kept at Brooklyn headquarters, and both cars were used exclusively by Judge Rutherford.

Rutherford loved to depict the clergy as money grubbers with their hands in the pockets of the people, and big business as greedy commercialists exploiting the workers. In fact, Rutherford was himself guilty of these very things. While his workers plodded from door to door selling his prolific writings, the Judge lived the life of a major industrialist. He spent the winters at Beth Sarim and traveled by steamship to Europe each summer. At Brooklyn headquarters he maintained a luxurious apartment on the top floor. All of this was done during the depression, when soup lines were the norm in America. Ironically, although Rutherford fashioned the organization into the "Fuller Brush" of religion, he himself never went door to door. The reason given was that he was too busy with executive responsibilities.[14]

The Judge had a prodigious appetite for alcoholic beverages and was not pleased when Prohibition became law. He railed against that law in a booklet entitled "Prohibition and the League of Nations." In it he said, "Let it be clearly understood that I am not advocating the violation of the Prohibition law."[15] Rutherford then proceeded to do just that when he had the Watch Tower's Canadian branch manager, W.F. Salter, illegally smuggle cases of whiskey, brandy, and other spirits across the border. Some years later, in a scathing letter to the Judge, a disillusioned Salter called Rutherford's lifestyle and consumption of liquor a "squandering of the Society's money."[16]

At a convention in 1931, Judge Rutherford announced a new name for the Bible Students—Jehovah's Witnesses. This name change had considerable impact. Since the schism of 1917 and the defections after the 1925 date failure, numerous small groups still referred to themselves as Bible Students. Rutherford labeled these the "Judas class" and "evil servants," and wished to differentiate them from the main Watch Tower group. He had already abandoned some of Russell's beliefs, including the pyramid teachings. Now with the name change he was ready to implement his autocratic "theocracy."

In the 1930's Jehovah's Witnesses were told that they did not have to submit to governmental authority. Rutherford based this on a radical reinterpretation of Romans 13. In this passage the apostle Paul writes that everyone must "be in subjection to the governing authorities." It is clear that Paul is talking about civil government, stating, "Because of this you also pay taxes, for rulers are servants of God" (Romans 13:6). Rutherford's new interpretation was that the authorities were *not* the political rulers and governments, but rather Jehovah God and His son, Jesus Christ! This doctrine remained in place until 1962, when the Society once again accepted the traditional Christian understanding of Romans 13. In the meantime it caused many problems for the Jehovah's Witnesses. Local laws often required permits for door-to-door distribution of literature. Using Rutherford's interpretation of Romans 13, they refused to obtain these permits, and so they were constantly in court.

A new gimmick was introduced in 1934—the use of portable phonographs which were manufactured by the Watch Tower and sold to Jehovah's Witnesses. The Witness would call at the door and present a short recording of Judge Rutherford. The object was to sell the householder a book at the conclusion of the message. In addition, automobiles equipped with loudspeakers cruised neighborhoods and blared out the Judge's diatribes, then invited people to come to a public discourse at some specified time and place.

As a result of all the various merchandising methods employed by the Watch Tower during this time, many clergymen, journalists, and others refered to it as a racket. Even some of Rutherford's followers became disenchanted, complaining, "This carrying books about is merely a book-selling scheme."[17] Not to be outdone, the Judge turned the tables and had Jehovah's Witnesses parade in front of churches on Sundays with placards bearing the slogan "RELIGION IS A SNARE AND A RACKET." This outraged the sensitivities of the public, and as a result persecution came upon Jehovah's Witnesses. On several occasions Witnesses were attacked by mobs and beaten or tarred and feathered.

A Rag, a Bone, and a Hank of Hair

The Judge's final convention appearance was a memorable one in St. Louis, Missouri, during August 1941. During one of his discourses he developed the thought that it was not only foolish but selfish for any Witness to marry because it kept a person from full-time service and would also result in "tribulation of the flesh." To drive home the point, the Judge, paraphrasing Kipling, said of women that they were nothing more than "a rag and a bone and a hank of hair." This statement encouraged the audience into a wild clapfest in which the women in attendance participated.[18] Rutherford reminded the crowd that Armageddon was just months away, and he drove home the idea that marrying and having children was an act of faithlessness for Jehovah's Witnesses.

At this convention a book entitled *Children* was released. It told a story about two faithful Witnesses named John and Eunice who, although deeply in love, would not marry because the storm of Armageddon was so close. They wanted to devote all their energies to the great work. They would serve the Lord now and wait to marry and have children in the New Order. Had John and Eunice been real people they would now be close to 70 years of age, still unmarried and awaiting Armageddon!

The authors have met several individuals who adopted this idea. More than once they and their intended mate went opposite directions to serve Jehovah in remote parts of the world and never saw each other again. In one case we asked an elderly gentleman why it was that he had remained single. His answer was that he wanted to serve the Lord and did not wish to "waste himself on women."

As with his predecessor, C. T. Russell, Judge Rutherford's wife left him. Mary and their son Malcolm moved to Los Angeles, California. In his book about the Witnesses entitled *Apocalypse Delayed*, M. James Penton reports that factors in their alienation included her poor health plus his "choleric and self-righteous temperament and what was quite evidently a serious case of alcoholism."[19]

Dr. Jerry Bergman, author of *The Mental Health of Jehovah's Witnesses*, related to us that during one of his many private conversations with the Watch Tower's attorney, Hayden C. Covington, he inquired, "Hayden, there are stories that Rutherford was a womanizer and had lady friends." Covington sat bolt upright. Leaning forward, he glared at Jerry and said: "If your wife was crippled and you were in the prime of your life, what would you have done?"

Could Rutherford and his followers justify such behavior? It could very well be, for he taught that all civil authorities and the clergy were of the devil and that therefore Witnesses did not need them in order to enter into a marriage relationship. Consequently, some Witnesses entered into consensual or common-law unions, which were considered quite acceptable by Rutherford.[20]

Final Wishes

Judge Rutherford died of bowel cancer on January 8, 1942, at Beth Sarim. His last wish was to be buried on the grounds of the San Diego mansion. A hue and a cry arose among the residents of the community, who were afraid that a cemetery in their exclusive district would have a detrimental effect on real estate values. Protracted hearings were held before the County Planning Commission and the Board of Supervisors of San Diego while Rutherford's body lay in a local mortuary. The argument was finally won in favor of the residents. Officially the Watch Tower Society states that three months after his death, Rutherford's body was shipped to New York and buried at Woodrow Cemetery on Staten Island. However, private rumor has it that the Judge was not denied his last eccentric wish.

Most Witnesses today are completely unaware of either the existence or significance of Beth Sarim. If it is mentioned at all by the Watch Tower Society, it is obliquely referred to as a winter getaway for President Rutherford because of his health. The house was quietly sold by the Watch Tower Society in 1948.

Concerning Beth Sarim, Rutherford once stated:

> The house has served as a testimony to many per-
> sons throughout the earth, and while the unbelievers
> have mocked concerning it and spoken contemptu-
> ously of it, yet it stands there as a testimony to Je-
> hovah's name. . . .[21]

The only testimony Beth Sarim ever gave was to presumptuous prophetic speculation and a colossal fraud.

What about the princes that were to occupy the mansion? The closet door was closed on that skeleton in 1950, when then-vice-president Fred W. Franz gave a speech entitled "New System of Things" during a convention at Yankee Stadium. He explained that the "Princes" were none other than those with leadership responsibilities within the congregations of Jehovah's Witnesses. With a few artfully contrived words, 57 years of Watch Tower prophetic speculation were put to rest!

Rutherford, though not an appointed Judge, acted the part by title and deed, while criticizing the clergy for their titles. He railed against the clergy for its class distinctions while himself exercising the control and rule of a Pope. He castigated the political arena while employing the tactics of a back-room poli-tico. His rhetoric was never without euphemisms attacking the "greedy commercialists" while himself leading a lifestyle that would make them envious. The Judge pointed his finger at a doomed world of decadent people while himself enjoying fine liquor, quality cigars, and the company of female traveling com-panions. He acted as a prophet of God predicting the end of the world and the resurrection of the Princes in 1925. He built a mansion to house the Princes upon their imminent return but was the only "Prince" to ever inhabit the home. Either Rutherford was a con man or else he had delusions that exceeded even Pastor Russell's. Probably the truth is that he possessed both of these traits.

4
The Watchtower Theocracy

Prophecy pays. There's no question that the heartbeat of the Watch Tower Bible and Tract Society is prophetic speculation. There is of course a negative impact when prophecy fails. However, even then, because of the system which the Watch Tower Society has in place, it can be (and is) a profitable experience overall. How so?

Historically, Jehovah's Witnesses defy the odds. It's true that after each prophetic failure, a noted decrease in membership occurred. However, it always rose again as a fresh wave of converts were convinced that the end was "just ahead." Most millenarian groups are not so fortunate.

Since the time of Christ, Christians have hoped for His second coming. Movements predicting specific dates for this momentous happening have not been rare. One of the earliest examples centered around Montanus, a "prophet" from Asia Minor in the second half of the second century. He preached the imminent second coming of Christ and the establishment of the New Jerusalem in Pepuza, Turkey. His message stressed prophecy and severe asceticism in immediate expectation of the Judgment Day. Although the predicted events did not take place, the movement did not end immediately. The Montanists continued a kind of Christianity of the elite until about 220 A.D., when the sect died out.

In the sixteenth century a leader by the name of Hoffman

predicted that the millennium would begin in 1533. He declared that Strassburg had been chosen as the New Jerusalem, which would be the center of the kingdom of righteousness where the 144,000 (spoken of in Revelation) would rule the earth. Many people believed Hoffman and began disposing of their worldly possessions, seeking to exemplify equality and brotherhood while seeking to win new converts. When 1533 came and went, this Anabaptist sect poured even more energy into proselytizing. Eventually they evolved into a less eschatologically centered movement. Today they form the historical roots of the Mennonites.

A third example is the Millerites in nineteenth-century America. William Miller was a New England farmer and Baptist minister. After an intensive two-year study of the Scriptures, he concluded that the end of the world would occur in 1843. He based his theory on a day-year transposition involving the so-called seven times of the Gentiles. Through lecture tours, a movement was organized. With Joshua V. Himes, Miller started a newspaper, *Signs of the Times*. When 1843 came and went, 1844 became the expected year of the second advent. Some believers were so convinced that the end was just ahead that they refused to plow their fields and plant crops. Miller and other Adventist leaders encouraged the followers to put aside normal activities in order to have more time to convert other people and spread the message.

The Millerite movement eventually disintegrated in controversy and dissension, breaking into several Adventist groups. The only survivor today is the group known as the Seventh-Day Adventists.

Each of these movements failed to last after the passing of its predicted date. In fact, few groups have survived even one failed date. Yet the Jehovah's Witnesses are going strong despite the failure of 1914, 1925, and 1975 plus a bevy of minor prophecies. What keeps them going? The answer is in the structure of the organization which took shape following the death of Judge Rutherford.

Governing Body

The Watch Tower Bible and Tract Society is no longer known for its charismatic leadership. Few people outside the Jehovah's Witnesses even know the name of the president. Rather than depending upon one individual to wield his powerful influence over the membership, the Society itself has become the center-piece for control. Today the direction of the Society issues from the Governing Body, made up of 13 men operating at the international headquarters in Brooklyn, New York.

The foundation for a new form of government was actually laid during Rutherford's presidency. He ended the presbyterial or democratic ruling system in local congregations and replaced it with his "theocratic" system. Supposedly God ruled the Jehovah's Witnesses—through the Judge.

Shortly before his death, Rutherford summoned his three closest aides to Beth Sarim and passed his mantle on to them. The men were Nathan Knorr, Hayden Covington, and Fred Franz. The battle for president was waged between Knorr and Covington, and Knorr won, supposedly because Covington confessed that he was not one of the anointed 144,000 ruling class. Covington then became vice-president.

The new president lacked both the personality and the charisma of his predecessors. He was an aloof and business-oriented individual. However, for the huge postwar expansion within the Watch Tower movement, Nathan Knorr was exactly the right man for the job. His forte was management. With his hands-on, brisk, executive approach, he had little time for researching and authoring the Society's publications. When asked a deep biblical question, he would reply "ask Freddie," referring to Fred Franz, who would eventually succeed Knorr as president in 1977. Knorr's vision called for total loyalty to a strong central organization. For that reason he instituted the policy that all Watch Tower literature would be published anonymously. This diluted the danger of personality factions.

The Witness community adopted a more believable posture during Knorr's presidency. Most of the outwardly eccentric practices were abandoned. Mass parades, sound cars, and insulting placards became history. Knorr instituted a training program in which Witnesses were taught to overcome objections with carefully rehearsed presentations. So the average Jehovah's Witness could now articulate his belief without the aid of a little "testimony" card or phonograph record. It all began to look respectable on the surface.

Global expansion also increased dramatically. In 1943 Knorr opened the Missionary School of Gilead. This was a place where eager young pioneers went for training in Watch Tower doctrine and—most important—Watch Tower policy. No matter where they went, the Society would operate by one set of rules. Knorr demanded absolute unity. He supervised the writing of an operations manual to be followed meticulously in every branch. There would be no adjustments for culture, no creativity, no individualism.

If Rutherford was the Fuller Brush man of religion, Knorr was its Iacocca. Overseers who had been trained at headquarters fanned out into the United States and the world to supervise activities and pore over the records, making sure that every local congregation tended to business. Every baptized Witness who was actively selling materials door to door submitted a monthly report. Quotas were set. Regions were mapped out. Everyone had an area to reach.

Another Witness trademark was the gigantic assemblies that were held each summer in arenas like Yankee Stadium. As many as 70,000 people or more would overflow the stands to hear the latest teaching and purchase the newest books and materials. These gatherings instilled pride in the expanding organization. They were also part of a massive educational program designed to train the rank-and-file membership to more effectively preach the message.

Brooklyn Heights became virtually a Witness anthill. Building after building—many of them historic old brownstones—was bought, then razed or modified with no thought to esthetic appeal or historical significance. Workers scurried through streets, up and down stairways and elevators, to and from various job assignments. Hundreds of people worked in the factory and office complexes, where an austere, no-nonsense, functional atmosphere prevailed. Great emphasis was placed on self-sufficiency. Staff members lived dormitory-style, with two, three, or four people occupying a simply furnished room. Most of the food consumed by workers at the Bethel factories and offices was produced at the Watch Tower farm near Wallkill, New York. The ink, glue, and paste used in the bindery was also produced by the Society. Other branches were set up around the world, each operating in the same manner as the headquarters.

Under Knorr's methodic leadership, growth was steady through the 40's, 50's, and early 60's. Yet there was little to make the organization stand out as it had earlier with its charismatic figureheads. Growth was slowing and literature sales stagnating. Something dramatic was needed.

The answer was a return to a more brazen form of prophetic speculation. For years Armageddon was "just around the corner" or "a few months or years away." But in 1966 the Society announced that the end of 6000 years of history would arrive in the fall of 1975. They didn't come right out and say that Christ's millennial reign would begin then, but they strongly suggested that 1975 would be an "appropriate" time for these events to occur.

The announcement was made in a book called *Life Everlasting in Freedom of the Sons of God.* This less-than-succinct title developed at great length where mankind was in the stream of time. It contained an elaborate chart of five pages, beginning with the creation of Adam in 4026 B.C., and listed all manner of historical dates as well as mundane dates significant only to the Watch Tower Society.[1] At the terminus date of 1975 the chart stated "End of 6th 1000-year day of man's existence (in early autumn)!" A heavy black line then separated the columns. The year 2975 appeared and the chart concluded with the following statement: "End of 7th 1000-year day of man's existence (in early autumn)."

All the chronology added up to one thing: Armageddon was close, within a decade! Adam's creation in 4026 B.C. plus 6000 years equaled 1975, plus the 1000-year reign of Christ equaled 2975, completing the seventh rest "day" of God. Therefore the end of the world, Armageddon, would have to take place by the fall of 1975! To squelch any doubts, page 29 declared:

> According to this trustworthy Bible chronology six thousand years from man's creation will end in 1975, and the seventh period of a thousand years of human history will begin in the fall of 1975.

The troops were told to go and spread the word, and throughout the next nine years the activity and increase was unparalleled in Watch Tower history. In 1965 the annual increase had dropped to 3.2 percent, but by 1974 the Society was enjoying an annual increase of 13.5 percent.[2] The number of active Witnesses in 1966, the year of the release of the *Life Everlasting* book, was 1,118,665. By 1975 the number had almost doubled, to 2,179,256![3]

It was a heady time, and literature sales soared to new heights. Studies with interested persons ran to all-time highs. Should a person not decide within six months to become a Jehovah's Witness, he was dropped. Before, studies had sometimes lasted two or three years, but now there was no time for the indecisive. Witnesses quit school, canceled insurance policies, and sold their homes and businesses. "Stay alive till 75" became a slogan. All of this life-altering activity did not spring just from the release of the *Life Everlasting* book, but rather was carefully fueled and orchestrated by the Watch Tower leadership during the years leading up to 1975.

For example, in 1967 *The Watchtower*, though adding a cautionary note, continued to emphasize how "reliable" the calculations from *Life Everlasting* were:

How much longer will it be, then, before God takes action to destroy the wicked and usher in the blessings of his Kingdom rule? Interestingly, the autumn of the year 1975 marks the end of 6,000 years of human experience. This is ascertainable from reliable chronology preserved in the Bible itself. What will that year mean for humankind? Will it be the time when God executes the wicked and starts off the thousand-year reign of his Son Jesus Christ? It very well could, but we will have to wait to see.[4]

In the monthly sales bulletin *Kingdom Ministry* there was much exhortation as to the nearness of 1975. An overlay of guilt drove Witnesses to expend themselves:

Just think, brothers, there are *only ninety months left* before 6,000 years of man's existence on earth is complete. . . . The majority of people living today will probably be alive when Armageddon breaks out, and there are no resurrection hopes for those who are destroyed then.[5]

An article in *The Watchtower* magazine reminded the reader how little time was left before Christ's millennial reign would begin:

The immediate future is certain to be filled with climactic events, for this old system is nearing its complete end. Within a few years at most the final parts of Bible prophecy relative to these "last days" will undergo fulfillment, resulting in the liberation of surviving mankind into Christ's glorious 1,000-year reign.[6]

These are but a few samples of what was steady fare for Witnesses of the period. Year in and year out, both from the platform and in the printed page, the thought that the millennium was at hand was emphasized.

But of course, 1975 came and went. Predictably, there was great disappointment. During the period 1976 through 1978 alone, approximately 390,000 Witnesses left the organization worldwide. Many others quietly voiced concerns. The rumbles reached all the way to the highest levels of the Society.

No doubt that was part of the reason why there was such a dramatic upheaval at Bethel headquarters. For some time a Governing Body had been in place, serving primarily as a rubber stamp for approval or resolution of various policy matters brought up by the president. That began to change in 1975. Several members of the Governing Body sought to assume more active control of the organization. Six committees were set up to oversee various aspects of Society operation. The result was a dramatic reorganization in which the Governing Body took over much of the authority exercised by the president. President Knorr reluctantly accepted the change. He died 18 months later and was succeeded by Fred Franz, who at the time was in his eighties. While he still carried influence in his position, no longer could he or any one man determine the direction of the Society.

Today the Governing Body is an autocratic council that rules with unchallenged authority. All policies, regulations, and doctrinal matters reside under the power and authority of these men. Every Witness is subject to their dictatorship from the cradle to the grave. This fact is of major importance in understanding the continued growth of Jehovah's Witnesses, for they consider the Governing Body as God's means of theocratic rule.

Theocracy Defined

A theocracy is a system of ecclesiastical rulership administered by the immediate direction of God. In ancient Israel this meant that God was recognized as the supreme civil Ruler and that His laws were taken as the law of the state. The law was administered by the priests and eventually by the kings of Israel.

In Judge Rutherford's thinking, Witness "theocracy" was equally well-defined. Jehovah's Witnesses were ruled by the supreme sovereign of the universe, Jehovah God Himself, through the president and officers of the Watch Tower Bible and Tract Society headquartered in Brooklyn, New York. On June 15, 1938, all congregations were presented with a resolution which said in part "that 'THE SOCIETY' is the visible representative of the Lord on earth." Almost without exception, the congregations adopted this resolution.[7] This amounted to a complete surrender of the democratic style of church control that had existed within the congregations of Jehovah's Witnesses for 60 years. It was the beginning of a control mechanism that has reached Orwellian proportions in modern times. The present-day Governing Body exercises absolute and complete control over the lives of Jehovah's Witnesses worldwide.

With all this awesome responsiblity over the lives of millions of Witnesses, one would imagine that this body of men would be deeply concerned about following biblical principles. Raymond Franz, a former member of the Governing Body (and nephew of the current president), says that this isn't the case. Franz had been a lifelong member of Jehovah's Witnesses, serving faithfully in a number of capacities down through the years. He was invited to become a member of the Governing Body in 1971 and considered it a supreme privilege at the time.

After nine years on the Governing Body, he had a very different perspective. In a personal interview he told us:

> I must say that it was one of the most disillusioning experiences of my life. I envisioned the Governing Body as a body of men to whom the Bible, God's Word, was the controlling force, and who, in every one of their decisions, really dug into the Scriptures to make sure that everything they did was soundly based upon the Bible. When I got into the Governing Body, I found that the Bible was rarely appealed to, was rarely used. Mainly it was a matter of discussing organizational policy, and how to apply this organizational

policy. And I found that again and again, when issues came up, even though Scriptures might be presented, if there was an organizational policy, that policy would take precedence over Scripture. I couldn't help but think of Jesus' words in Matthew 23, that they have made the Word of God null and void because of their tradition.

Indeed, Matthew 23 describes perfectly the Governing Body of Jehovah's Witnesses. Jesus called the scribes and Pharisees blind guides, denying their followers access to heaven. Jesus held them accountable because their traditions and teachings kept people away from Him. Moreover, the scribes and Pharisees weighed down the people with rules and regulations that were extrabiblical.

The story of Ray Franz shows how hard it is to fight the tide of such a group. Driven by his conscience and a desire to follow what the Bible teaches, he frequently found himself opposing the majority decisions. When he privately questioned some of the Society's doctrines with close friends, word got back to the body that he was a traitor. Though he publicly supported the Society's positions, he was forced to resign from the Governing Body in 1980 and ordered to leave the headquarters. A year later he was disfellowshipped for eating a meal with a former Jehovah's Witness who had disassociated himself from the organization. Ray told his story in detail in a book titled *Crisis of Conscience.*

The Governing Body is composed of elderly men, some of whom have never married. Of those who are married, most have not had children. They live a cloistered existence at Watch Tower headquarters, with their everyday needs cared for by others. Yet they dictate the lives of their followers in the most minute detail, even though they have little experience in intimate family matters or of life in the outside world. The average Witness would not recognize most Governing Body members if he were to see them on the street, much less know their names. How can this shadowy group of men have such control? How can it be that their ever-changing pharisaical rules and doctrines can be imposed upon millions of men and women? On what authority do they base their control?

The answer is in the Society's teaching of theocracy. The Watch Tower Society claims that Jesus Christ began to reign invisibly in 1914. He needed an organization to announce His kingdom and administer His interests. They claim that in 1919 Christ carefully examined all the Christian religions but rejected them in favor of the Watch Tower Society. The Governing Body supposedly has been given jurisdiction over the Lord's organization in order to maintain its doctrinal purity. In this way the Society has established the ultimate mind control. To establish an elite class of leaders whose teachings and doctrines cannot be questioned is the first step into cultism. Jehovah's Witnesses took that step long ago.

The Watch Tower Society bases the authority of its Governing Body on the words of Jesus in Matthew 24:45—"Who then is the faithful and sensible slave ['faithful and discreet slave,' according to the Society's *New World Translation*], whom his master put in charge of his household to give them their food at the proper time?"

It is important to carefully examine this teaching. If the "faithful and discreet slave" doctrine is a myth and the 1919 appointment of the "slave" by Jesus Christ is a carefully contrived fabrication, then the authority claimed by the Governing Body of Jehovah's Witnesses is nothing short of blasphemy.

Royal Appointment

Jehovah's Witnesses believe that when Jesus spoke of a "faithful and discreet slave," He was referring to a class of persons totaling 144,000 that is spoken of in Revelation 7 and 14. They believe that a remnant of this 144,000 gathered together under the direction of Christ in the late nineteenth century to prepare themselves for Christ's return and inspection. But was this always the view? Charles Taze Russell held this view until 1896, when he assumed the position and title of the "faithful and wise servant" for himself. This was the official doctrine until 1927, when Judge Rutherford changed it back to a class of 144,000 people.

This is not a mere example of doctrinal vacillation, but is in fact crucial to Society theology. Today the Watch Tower claims that Jesus Christ inspected their organization in 1919 and found a "faithful and discreet slave" *class* dispensing fine spiritual food to true believers.[8]

Did Jesus actually find a class of persons who recognized themselves as this "slave" class? In 1919, even though Russell had been dead for three years, the Bible Students still looked to him as that "servant" or "slave." So, according to Watch Tower history, Jesus would have found a dead man serving as the "faithful and wise servant!"

Today the Watch Tower leadership points to early writings of Russell to show that he taught that the "servant" was a class of individuals, and that Russell never claimed to be that servant.[9] They use publications prior to 1896 for this cover-up. They neglect to reveal Russell's change of view from a class to an individual, yet the evidence is overwhelming that this concept was held by the Bible Students. This was apparent in Russell's writings as early as 1897, in *The Battle of Armageddon*, Vol. IV, page 613, in which he stressed "servant" in the singular. In a biography of Pastor Russell published in the years 1924 through 1927, the Watch Tower Society proclaimed Russell as "that faithful and wise servant" chosen by the Lord.[10]

Though Russell had been dead since 1916, the 1927 edition of *The Finished Mystery* stated on page 144, "Though Pastor Russell has passed beyond the veil, he is still managing every feature of the Harvest work." The Watch Tower Society's official history book admits, "It was the published and accepted thought down till 1927 that he was 'that servant' of Matthew 24:45."[11] So Charles Taze Russell was the "faithful and discreet slave" even though he was dead! Just how he transmitted the "food in due season" to his followers and managed every feature of the harvest work has never been revealed by the Watch Tower.

One year after Russell's death, in the lead article in *The Watch Tower* of November 1, 1917, entitled "A Tribute to the Seventh Messenger," his role was emphatically stressed:

> The Lord Jesus in his great prophetic statement in Matthew 24:45-47, made known the fact that at the end of the age he would be present and would have a special servant whom he would "make ruler over all his house to give meat in due season to the household." ... For several years some have recognized, and now many more are recognizing, that Pastor Russell is that servant. ... Pastor Russell is the servant promised to the church in the closing days of its earthly pilgrimage.[12]

To further his concept of a theocratic organization, Rutherford realized that he had to dethrone Russell as "God's mouthpiece." The "servant," in a chameleonlike move, became a class of individuals once again, with Rutherford at the head of the class.

The importance of this change is the fact that the Watch Tower Society today claims that when Jesus Christ made His final inspection in 1919, he found a "faithful and discreet slave class," a group of individuals dispensing spiritual food. But in fact Russell alone was considered the "servant" or "slave" during that time period.

Meat in Due Season?

Christ's appointment of the Watch Tower Society was supposedly also based on an understanding of doctrinal matters—that is, the quality of the spiritual food or teachings that the "slave" was serving when Jesus made His inspection.[13] We can examine the material the Watch Tower was serving in the

1918-19 time period, for indeed the spiritual food was dispensed by way of the printed page.

The Finished Mystery, printed in 1917, was the latest food hot out of the oven. The following are some of the book's teachings that Jesus Christ would have inspected when He was supposedly choosing the organization that would be His representatives on earth:

- In 1918 God would destroy the churches and church members by the millions, and Christendom would go down into oblivion in that year.
- There would be worldwide anarchy in the fall of 1920.
- God's kingdom would be established in 1931.
- The Lord's second advent had taken place in 1874.
- Behemoth of Job 40:15ff. was the stationary steam engine. Its loins were the boiler plates and its tail the smokestack.
- Leviathan of Job 41:1ff. was the steam locomotive and its tongue was the coupling-link. Its soft tones were the locomotive's whistle.
- The sleeping saints were resurrected in 1878.
- In 1918 demons would invade the minds of the church members of Christendom (referred to as "the swine class") and cause them to engage in things that would lead the enraged masses to destroy them.
- Revelation 9:13 mentions a voice, and that was the voice of William Miller, the Adventist, from 1829 to 1844.
- The "little flock" of Bible Students then alive would be glorified in 1918.
- The "man child" of Revelation 12:5 was the Roman Catholic papacy.
- Michael and his angels mentioned in Revelation 12:7 were the Pope of Rome and his bishops.
- The publishing of *The Finished Mystery* was foretold in Revelation 14:20, where the 1600 furlongs represent the distance from where it was authored in Scranton, Pennsylvania, to Watch Tower headquarters in Brooklyn, New

York—provided you traveled by way of the Lackawanna Railroad and the Hoboken Ferry!
• The seven volumes of *Studies in the Scriptures* were the Seven angels of Revelation 15:1.
• The Lord assumed an interest in and responsibility for the complete series of *Studies in the Scriptures*.

There is an axiom that the best defense is a good offense. The modern Watch Tower Society has employed this principle in its cover-up of the facts concerning the "spiritual food" that the "slave" was dispensing at that crucial time period when Jesus Christ was supposedly inspecting them. The leaders discourage their membership from reading older material. Their rationale is that the "light" gets brighter as time goes on. Therefore older material is "old light." Although *The Finished Mystery* was printed until 1927 and distributed for years afterward, the average Jehovah's Witness is not aware of its contents nor the deceitful way in which the Watch Tower organization presents it.

Ambassadors of the Kingdom

Another important feature claimed in connection with the Society's appointment in 1919 concerns their ambassadorial responsibility. They claim that Jehovah's Witnesses recognized the birth of God's kingdom in 1914 and have been announcing it ever since that date:

> "This good news of the kingdom will be preached in all the inhabited earth for a witness to all the nations; and then the end will come." (Matt. 24:7-14) Has God's Messianic kingdom been having that done on earth since 1914? Have the Gentile nations been receiving this Kingdom witness? Yes![14]

What the leadership neglects to tell its followers is that in 1919 the Watch Tower Society taught that the time of the end began in

1799, that the Lord returned invisibly in 1874—*not* 1914!—and that the end of the age, which failed to come in 1914, was now to happen in 1925! In fact, a full ten years later the 1929 book *Prophecy*, written by Rutherford, said the following on page 65:

> The Scriptural proof is that the second presence of the Lord Jesus Christ began in 1874 A.D.

The importance of the "appointment" doctrine and the 1914 date is central to the whole theological system of Jehovah's Witnesses. If these two concepts can be dislodged, the entire system falls like a house of cards. That is why both concepts are constantly stressed to the Witnesses. It is also why the Watch Tower organization forbids Witnesses to speak to former members and other knowledgeable persons concerning these matters.

The idea that Matthew 24:45 refers to an appointment by Jesus of an earthly organization at a given moment in time has no foundation in fact. The passage is a parable, as traditional Bible commentaries have recognized for centuries. The Watch Tower's interpretation tortures the rules of biblical hermeneutics and exegesis. Moreover, in Matthew 25:20-23, in the Parable of the Talents, there is reference to more than one faithful and discreet slave! The Master calls both the servant who invested five talents and the servant who invested two talents "good and faithful." The two parables are pictures of Christ's kingdom and the responsibility which *all* individuals have within His kingdom.

The Watch Tower official version of what took place in 1919 is that Jesus Christ examined all the Christian organizations and societies, including those that had been established for centuries, and found them unqualified. The Watch Tower Society was chosen because they, and they alone, manifested the characteristics of the "faithful and discreet slave." Today they claim that they were acting as ambassadors, announcing the newly established kingdom in 1914 and warning the world that it had entered its time of the end in that same year. In actual fact, in 1919 the Watch Tower Society was still teaching that the "time of the end" had begun in 1799 and that Jesus Christ had come invisibly in 1874 and set up His kingdom. They were in a state of confusion concerning 1914; they were "ambassadors" announcing a date 40 years earlier than they now claim.

Today the Watch Tower claims that Jesus Christ would have inspected the quality of "food" that the "slave" was dispensing and this would be most important in His decision-making process. But in 1919 the Watch Tower Society's latest spiritual food was that contained in *The Finished Mystery*. This book and the rest of the *Studies in the Scriptures* were used at that time as the basis for Watch Tower teaching. The *Studies* emphasized dates which the current Watch Tower now rejects. Moreover, these books endorsed the pyramid teaching which Rutherford finally renounced a decade after Jesus Christ supposedly approved it as "quality spiritual food."

The Watch Tower would have the world believe that Jesus Christ also chose them because of their keen understanding of the "times and seasons." In fact, all their dates had proven false up to that point, yet they had gone on to new prophetic speculation at the very time Jesus Christ was supposedly examining them! "Millions now living will never die" was the message of the day, and the end was set for 1925, when Abraham, Isaac, Jacob, and the other ancient worthies were to be resurrected.

Certainly Jesus Christ would know that these things were not going to take place in 1925. It is incredible to believe that He would nevertheless go ahead and choose the Watch Tower organization in spite of their track record of false prophecy.

When we examine the beliefs, dates, and spiritual food, as well as who the "slave" was at that critical time, how could Jesus Christ possibly have picked the Watch Tower organization? The question becomes even more valid when we consider that what the Watch Tower teaches today is 180 degrees opposite to what they taught then. If they were correct then and Jesus chose them, He would have to abandon them now, because their belief system is totally reversed. If they are correct now, they were therefore wrong then, so on what basis were they chosen? Either way, the teaching of the appointment of the "faithful and discreet slave" and "wise servant" class is unfounded.

Unfortunately, millions of Jehovah's Witnesses believe this teaching. The Watch Tower leadership is guilty of a terrible deception that is entrapping and enslaving their followers.

We understand how people can be so trapped, for that is what we were for 22 years. We accepted Watch Tower teaching in total and gave our lives to the spread of its message. Everything in our family, our business, and our friendships revolved around the organization. We accepted every edict from headquarters as spiritual food sent directly from God. Only toward the end did we realize that we had been terribly deceived.

5

Finding True Freedom in Jesus Christ

It was the first of a series of conventions that were held during the summer of 1966 throughout Canada. At the Exhibition grounds in Toronto, more than 30,000 Jehovah's Witnesses had sat through three-plus days of teaching, highlighted by two dramatic presentations about the Old Testament prophet Jeremiah and the modern-day application of the Bible.

Now, this Saturday afternoon, June 25, the speaker presented a powerful message about the freedom and liberty which God's sons have to carry out the great work of preaching God's kingdom, and how important it was that this message be spread—now more than ever, for there was no question that the end of time as we knew it was approaching.

We were part of that throng in June of 1966, and we had heard such exhortations before. But this was different. The speaker was presenting new chronology, fresh evidence that proved that Armageddon was approaching. It was all based on the teaching that the seven days in Genesis, during which God created the earth, actually consisted of seven 7000-year weeks. When God rested after His creation of Adam and Eve, that began the seventh 7000-year week, consisting of seven 1000-year days. Of those 7000 years, the final 1000 would be the millennium. Calculating from the supposed date of Adam's creation, the first 6000 years were coming to a close. And it was all spelled out in the new Society book: *Life Everlasting—In Freedom of the Sons of God.*

Stationed throughout the stadium were people with cases of the publication. As soon as the program was over, the audience

69

thronged around the sellers to purchase the new book. As we ate our dinner and waited for the evening program to start, people throughout the arena were thumbing through the text. We shared in the excitement as we turned to page 31 of the book. There it was—a chart showing the key events of man's history, beginning with Adam's creation in 4026. Over the next five pages we observed the chronology. The current year, 1966, was noted: "Threat of World War III grows more ominous . . ." and "Expansion of organization of Jehovah's Christian witnesses continues." Next to the date was the number of years since Adam's creation—5991.

Below that notation was the line that had all of us excited. The date: 1975. Years from Adam's creation: 6000. Event: End of sixth 1000-year day of man's existence (in early autumn).

This was it! The great event we had so longed for was just nine years away! The end was near. Jehovah would rain His judgment on the earth, and only we, His chosen organization, would survive to enjoy the 1000-year millennial paradise.

Of course, there was a lot of work to do before then, but we were willing to work. After all, if Jehovah had shown such compassion on us, it was reasonable that we should work hard to bring as many people into His ark of protection—His chosen organization—before the end. This was just the motivation we needed to redouble our efforts.

That is not to say we weren't working hard already. Since our baptism in 1960, the two of us had been diligent publishers—the Society's name for those who go door to door every week to spread the good news—and attended all the required meetings.

Our observation is that generally three basic types of people tend to get involved with Jehovah's Witnesses. There are those who are born into the religion—like our daughter Lorraine—and have no choice. There are the Bible illiterates—perhaps as much as 65 percent of Society membership—who come from churches, but who have no ability to defend their faith and so fall victim to the aggressive Witness pitch. And third, there are those who are predisposed—those basically decent people with little or no religious background who have no basic prejudices against religion.

We fell into the third category. As a boy, Leonard had a penchant for religious things. Whenever he visited his grandmother in Montreal, he went with her to church. His father was an agnostic, but his mother had a desire to know more about God. When Leonard moved to Toronto, he met Pat Condon and they became the closest of friends through high school. Pat's parents were studying with the Witnesses, and on occasion Pat's father told Leonard what they were learning. It made a lot of logical sense, especially compared to what Leonard understood about Christianity. For example, he could not accept the concept of hell, and the Jehovah's Witnesses did not believe in hell. He remembers well the banner they mounted across their house one summer: "IT'S LATER THAN YOU THINK."

Marjorie had a little more Witness influence in her home. Her mother had studied for several years with the Witnesses, and after she and her husband bought an old estate, she began holding weekly lectures. On those occasions when she could not find a speaker, she would play old records of Judge Rutherford for her invited guests.

We met after high school. Leonard decided against college and went to work in the graphic arts field. This provided the finances for his real love—cars. After attending Guelph Business College, Marjorie began working full-time in a business office and met Leonard when her brother Bill brought him up for a weekend in the country. We began to date not long after.

Naturally, our Witness exposure was discussed during our dating. One evening after we were engaged, we talked about our goals as we drove Leonard's Chevy convertible along Lakeshore Drive. We both agreed that there was something worth checking out in the Jehovah's Witnesses. And if it was God's organization, and it was true that Armageddon was just around the corner, we needed to become committed.

We were married on May 19, 1956, and rented a little cottage in a suburb of Toronto. The only problem with the home was that there were no facilities for Leonard to wash his car. One Sunday morning Leonard drove over to his parents' house to wash his car, and who should come by but a Jehovah's Witness, asking if Leonard wanted to renew his subscription to the *Watchtower*. The truth was that the Condon family had given him the subscription, and Leonard had two or three years worth of back issues stacked up, still in their brown mailing wrappers, unread. However, Leonard renewed the subscription, giving the Witness his new address. As he was leaving, the Witness told Leonard that there would be a public discourse at the Kingdom Hall. The subject was one of interest to Leonard—the Bible versus evolution.

We attended that lecture and were most impressed. The talk was one that could be given to any Christian group. It clearly showed how the Genesis account stands up against evolution. It made a lot of sense and we agreed that it was a powerful message. After the talk, Leonard went forward to talk to the speaker and asked, "How do you go about getting one of those home Bible studies in your home?"

And so we began studying the teachings of the Jehovah's Witnesses. We took our time, asking questions and wrestling with things that bothered us. On occasion we went out to observe door-to-door witnessing when we were invited. We knew the seriousness of a commitment and were in no rush to make such an important decision.

After our daughter was born in 1957, we moved back into Toronto so Leonard could be closer to work. The Kingdom Hall we had visited sent our address to a nearby congregation and we were visited by Fred and Ruth McDowell. The only way to describe them is fanatic. They were zealots for the Watch Tower Society. There was a constant sense of urgency about their work that affected us. Since they happened to have a child the same age as Lorraine, we became friends. At the McDowells' urging, we were baptized in 1960.

Now that we were committed, we diligently put in our hours of service as congregation publishers, doing at least ten hours of door-to-door witnessing every month. The schedule was full: Tuesday and Thursday night and Sunday meetings. Wednesday nights were used for Bible study in the home of a potential Witness. Fridays were devoted to personal study of Watchtower materials in preparation for the Sunday meeting. On Saturday mornings Leonard did his door-to-door work, while Marge found time to do it during the week.

Soon Leonard was being considered for a position as an assistant, as ministerial servants were called then. While he wasn't actively seeking the position, Leonard was surprised when all of a sudden he was dropped from consideration without a word of explanation. Only later did he learn that another member of the congregation had heard Leonard express a word of skepticism about some Watchtower teaching and had reported it. It was several years before he again was considered for such a position. That should have served as a warning for us of the problems we would soon see so clearly in the organization.

Another major decision concerned having children. Our daughter was born with RH-positive blood. Since Marjorie's blood is RH-negative, this meant that her body was now sensitized with antibodies against any subsequent RH-positive baby she would bear. Women with RH-negative blood routinely received a gamma globulin shot immediately following giving birth in order to insure against such problems in subsequent children. But Witness women were not allowed to take this shot because the serum was made from the blood of a sensitized woman.

At this time the Toronto newspapers often had headlines about blood transfusion cases involving Witness babies whose mothers had the same condition as Marjorie's. Typically, child welfare authorities would declare the parents unfit, take custody of the infant, do a blood transfusion, and then place the baby in foster care until he recovered. Only then would parents regain custody of their child.

To thwart the authorities, Witnesses often urged parents to kidnap their baby from the hospital and hide it until the child either recovered from its jaundiced condition or died. We were not prepared to put ourselves or our child through such trauma and so decided not to have any more children. (It was not until June 1974 that Watchtower leadership reversed itself and gave permission for Witness women to accept gamma globulin injections. But it was too late for Marjorie. Lorraine was to be married in two months, and Armageddon was due to come the following year!)

Meanwhile, our one child found life in a Witness family difficult. We did what we could to make her life enjoyable, but like all Witness children, she had to sit through the long Kingdom Hall meetings, and she was not allowed to have any non-Witness friends at school or in the neighborhood. School was the hardest for her. Often she was the only Witness child in her class, and she would frequently cry before she left home in the morning. The Society strictly forbids members from saluting the flag or participating in the pledge of allegiance or prayer before school or at other meetings. Lorraine had to stay seated or else stand out in the hall while the other students participated in these activities. We hated ourselves for making her endure this, for we knew that adult Witnesses carefully avoided any situation where we might have to take such a stand. Yet we expected a little child to face this every day. Finally, in the fourth grade, she had a teacher who took a special interest in her and made her feel important. But overall she suffered a very lonely life.

Shortly before the great Toronto assembly in 1966, Leonard started an advertising display business. Among his customers was Procter and Gamble. We now found ourselves financially better off then we had ever been before. Perhaps if there hadn't been the anticipation concerning 1975, he might have been more aggressive concerning long-term planning and expansion. Instead, we sold the business in 1972 in order to devote more effort to preparing for Armageddon. Two years later we sold our home. At a time when we were at our peak professionally, we were pulling back.

"Stay alive until '75" became the rallying cry of the Witnesses. It affected all of our lives in many ways. All of our decisions—family, career, education, hobbies—were made in light of this date. In many ways we felt we were living life on hold. Many of our interests would have to wait until the "New Order" arrived. One's time had to be spent in door-to-door work or in preparation for meetings at the Kingdom Hall.

As a young woman, Marjorie had been an avid reader with a well-worn library card. On becoming a Witness, she gave that up. She felt guilty reading non-Witness material when there was so much Witness material to study. In her early thirties she started taking a course at a local design college. It didn't interfere with her meeting attendance or door-to-door work, yet she quickly became a "marked" person in the congregation. After six months of "silent treatment" she gave up the schooling.

The stress of living up to these expectations took its toll on Marjorie's health. She developed a severe gastric stomach, and was tested for an ulcer. There was never enough time to relax and unwind. You felt guilty if you took a few hours to listen to music or read a good book. That was valuable time which could be spent making more calls or doing some return visits to homes that had bought Watchtower literature from you.

The pressure was even worse for Leonard after he became an elder. In addition to all the regular requirements, he had to prepare discourses to present to the congregation, and there were additional evenings and weekends spent counseling with congregation members who had problems. There was little time in his mad schedule for talking to his own family or attending to the needs of a wife and child. Over and over we were reminded in Society publications what a joy it was to be involved in Kingdom work. Though few people openly admitted it, from our observation there weren't too many who seemed to experience the joy of service to Jehovah.

It was the promise of 1975 that kept us motivated. We were told that Bible studies with prospective Witnesses must be limited to six months in order to use our time in the most effective way possible; those who didn't respond were to be dropped.[1]

Those (like us) who sold their homes and businesses in order to spend their time proclaiming the end were commended. "Certainly this is a fine way to spend the short time remaining before the wicked world's end," we read.[2] Others chose to remain childless so that they would be less encumbered in preaching the news of God's kingdom.[3] We were constantly reminded of the approaching end, and it governed all our decisions.

For example, our daughter told us she wanted to get married in 1974, even though she was only 17. We weren't very pleased with the idea, and neither were her fiancé's parents. But her fiancé was a Jehovah's Witness. And since Armageddon was just a year away, we gave our consent.

Of course, when 1975 passed into 1976, there was a great deal of disappointment. Leadership assured us that the end wasn't far off. It was a matter of weeks or months—not years. Most of us were willing to wait another year. But when 1976 passed, everyone could sense the dissension building. Some people had already left and more were thinking about it. And that was the catalyst for members to start questioning other Society policies and doctrine.

One might expect that the leadership would finally admit that they were in error concerning 1975. Instead, they did nothing to alleviate these feelings. In fact, in a rather cavalier fashion they dismissed the matter and chastised us for our zeal.

In the July 15, 1976, issue of *Watchtower* we read:

It may be that some who have been serving God have planned their lives according to a mistaken view of just what was to happen on a certain date or in a certain year. They may have, for this reason, put off or neglected things that they otherwise would have cared for. But they have missed the point of the Bible's warnings concerning the end of this system of things, thinking that Bible chronology reveals the specific date. . . . If anyone has been disappointed through not following this line of thought, he should now concentrate on adjusting his viewpoint, seeing that it was not the word of God that failed or deceived him and brought disappointment, but that his own understanding was based on wrong premises.[4]

At about this same time we attended a large Witness gathering at a new assembly hall in Georgetown, a small town northwest of Toronto. The then-vice-president F.W. Franz gave a convoluted discourse which ultimately led to the point of his visit and talk. He asked the audience in a shrill manner, "Do you know why nothing happened in 1975?" After a rather protracted pause he virtually shouted a reply to his question: "It was because *you* expected something to happen!" He emphasized his point by waving his hand toward the audience in a theatrical style. We looked at each other in amazement, and you could have heard a pin drop in that large building holding thousands of Witnesses.

Naturally, that didn't sit well with us or with most Witnesses. In 1977, for the first time we could remember, there was a slight *decrease* in membership (about 1 percent). Still, we were willing to wait a little longer. However, we were tired of the harsh Toronto winters. We felt that if we had to wait a little longer for Armageddon, we might as well wait in a nicer climate. Besides, with Leonard's business sold and our daughter now married, there was no physical reason for us to stay put. So we packed up and moved to La Jolla, just north of San Diego.

When an elder moves, a letter of recommendation from his congregation goes with him. So Leonard immediately was appointed as an elder at the local Kingdom Hall. We found that the new congregation was in just as much of an uproar as the one we left in Canada. It was obvious that the Society's leadership needed to do something to calm the storm.

In 1977 the headquarters in Brooklyn sent Harley Miller out to speak to all the congregations in the San Diego area. Instead of our normal Kingdom Hall meetings that Sunday, we all assembled at the Del Mar Fairgrounds to hear Harley's talk. At first, when he brought up 1975, it appeared that he was trying to waffle and squirm his way out of the issue. Then suddenly he became very aggressive. In a bombastic manner he told about driving into the Fairgrounds that day and noticing the large palm tree that was prominently planted near the entrance. Pointing with dramatic emphasis toward that tree, he announced, "Anyone here in the audience who doesn't like what did or did not happen in 1975, I suggest you go out under that palm tree and cry about it."

The statement was shocking, and obviously meant to intimidate people who were used to blind obedience to the organization. But we weren't buying it. Marjorie was furious and whispered to Leonard, "I've had it. Let's go!" Leonard wanted to leave. However, we were seated in the front row, and there was no way we could have left without creating a scene. Maybe we should have left then, but we didn't. But from that point on, things changed.

It wasn't so much that we were upset with the date failure; we were disturbed with the way it was handled. It was like finding an empty cookie jar and seeing your child covered with cookie crumbs, yet when you ask him, "Did you eat those cookies?" he adamantly insists he did not. You expect such behavior from children, but we did not expect grown men to gloss over the truth and twist the fact to the point that many Jehovah's Witnesses began to doubt themselves. Maybe they had misinterpreted the message. Maybe it was their own fault for reading too much into the Watchtower publications.

We weren't buying it. It was there in black and white. For nine years they had carefully led us to believe that Armageddon could be expected to occur in 1975. Now they refused to accept responsibility for their statements. In our minds we thought of Jesus and how the disciples asked Him if it was time for the kingdom to be restored. He didn't belittle them for asking that question, but gently told them, "It is not for you to know times or epochs which the Father has fixed by His own authority; but you shall receive power when the Holy Spirit has come upon you" (Acts 1:7,8). There was no tenderness in the attitude of our leaders. These men, who were supposed to feed and care for the sheep, were instead ripping us to shreds.

Each of us went through various experiences in subsequent months that served to further erode our confidence in the organization. For Marjorie there were three specific events that were critical in her thinking. The first was an article she read in *Good Housekeeping* that listed all the 1500 religions in America. Near the top of the alphabetical list were the Adventists, and under them, as a subgroup, were Jehovah's Witnesses and perhaps another 10 or 12 "breakaway" groups under the Witnesses. Marjorie wondered why Witnesses were listed under the Adventists. And she had never heard of any breakaway groups; she thought we were united. Why had certain groups broken away? she wondered.

The second disconcerting event was the mass suicide in Jonestown, Guyana, that claimed more than 900 lives. These people died for a leader who was a false prophet. They died for a lie. Marjorie had always been willing to die, if need be, for the organization. But how was that attitude different from the followers of Jim Jones? Would she be dying for the truth? She wasn't sure anymore.

The third event was the arrival of our copy of the 1979 Yearbook put out by the Watchtower Society. Marjorie dutifully started reading the book. There was a section about Burma, and she noted that from the beginning of the work until 1965—a period of some 50 years—there had been very little growth. In 1965 the Society recorded only 270 publishers in Burma. But after 1966 the work started to grow. By 1975 there were 822 publishers, a 300 percent increase. But in 1977 there was a 1 percent drop. The article explained that the reason for the drop was because events did not occur as expected in 1975.

That statement hit Marjorie hard. Once again the leadership of the Watchtower was not humble enough to admit they had made a mistake: This was *not* their fault! Obviously Burma had gotten the message.

After reading that statistic, spontaneously a heartfelt prayer poured out to God: "Jehovah, I still believe this is the truth. I believe this is the one true religion. No matter what, I will serve You as faithfully as I know how. But if this religion is not the truth, the only way I will know it is if You show me. Please show me the truth." That prayer was answered five weeks later.

It was a Saturday, and Leonard was attending a quarterly elders' meeting—a time to review the condition of the local congregation. Several of the men had arrived early and were engaged in small talk. One of the elders, Jim, started telling Leonard about how the previous Thursday evening one of the brothers had brought him a manila envelope that had been mailed to him at his home. He said it was "from the apostates" and gave it to Jim. "I didn't open it or read it," the man told Jim. The elder commended the brother for his action.

"What do you mean you commended him for that?" Leonard asked Jim. "If we have the truth, we should be able to blow that stuff away."

Jim soberly shook his head. "I don't know," he answered. "I've read it over, and it's not so easy to blow this away."

Jim had the envelope with him, so Leonard said, "Let me have that. I want to see what these people are saying."

Recently there had been a growing concern among the leadership of the Society about former Jehovah's Witnesses who had left the organization and were now speaking out against the Society. The Society was trying to discredit these former members, calling them apostates because they were no longer "in the truth." They urged Witnesses to have nothing to do with them.

After the elders' meeting, Leonard returned home and immediately examined the material in the envelope. It was a 13-page $8^{1}/_{2}$ by 14 document with nothing but questions. Questions about failed prophecies. Questions about Society doctrines. Questions about Watchtower policies. Questions about why teachings are reversed 180 degrees, and then reversed back. Questions about quirky practices. Questions about the 144,000. Questions about chronology. And most important to Leonard—questions about credibility.

It was a disquieting list. Many of the questions were ones Leonard had asked himself but of course had never expressed aloud to any other Witnesses.

Wives of elders are only told about elder business on a "need to know" basis. Normally Leonard would not have shown Marge this material. But this was different. "Here, read this," he said, handing her the packet.

Marjorie felt her knees shake as she started to read the questions. Rank-and-file Witnesses were never allowed to read any religious material critical of the Society. But her nervousness stopped as she remembered her prayer. Perhaps this was God's answer.

That day we turned from being committed Witnesses to skeptics. We would continue to serve in the congregation, but now we were searching for the truth. This meant evaluating all that we had been taught during our years in the organization. We started challenging what we read, not just accepting it as inspired by God. Of course, we couldn't talk about this with our friends. But we were united as a couple in this quest for truth.

For the next year, after reading the list of questions, Marjorie attended Kingdom Hall meetings but was no longer going door to door. This was highly unusual behavior for the wife of a presiding overseer, yet no one confronted us with it.

Part of Leonard's duties as a congregational elder included speaking on occasion at other Kingdom Halls. He had about ten talks he had developed for this purpose, and they were quite popular. The message he liked most was on the life and death of Christ. This talk centered on the work of Christ in our life and salvation. One day Leonard informed the coordinator of these exchange talks that he would no longer give any talks except the one about the life and death of Christ.

Soon afterward Leonard was addressing an assembly in Escondido. In the midst of his message he had a strange experience—one that is hard to describe. It was as though for a brief moment the congregation was transformed before his eyes and Leonard saw them as a gray, faceless, beaten-down group of people. It was a momentary flash that only lasted a second, and he continued his talk without any interruption. But that moment stayed with him. It was though he had a new insight into the lives of Jehovah's Witnesses. We were an oppressed people.

Though we still didn't recognize Jesus Christ as deity, Leonard's talk was paving the way for the day when we would recognize Him as God and surrender our lives to Him. There was power in His name, where the organization had no spiritual power. Jesus Christ could change lives; the organization could only try to make people conform to a set of rules.

About two o'clock one morning Leonard received a phone call from a young woman who was living with her aunt, a member of our congregation. This woman had spent some time in the Peace Corps, and her experiences had left her with a nervous condition. She regularly took some prescription medication to control it. Since she was studying Witness teaching with her aunt and attended some of our Kingdom Hall meetings, one of the elders felt free to tell her that she should not be taking that drug—it was "pharmakia" and prohibited in the Bible. So she stopped taking the medication.

The elder was not a physician and had no idea what he was saying. The woman now had her aunt and other family members cornered in the kitchen with a butcher knife. The aunt had convinced her niece to talk to "Brother Chretien." Leonard quickly learned that she was not taking her medication and urged her to do so immediately. But the woman was hysterical and unable to follow any commands.

Then suddenly, in a move so totally unlike what we knew as Witnesses, Leonard said to this woman, "Jesus loves you."

Instantly the woman calmed down and began sobbing quietly. Whatever power had gripped her was gone. Marjorie, lying half-asleep, overheard Leonard's end of the conversation, and when he said those words her eyes opened wide. Those words were simply not ones we used!

In the summer of 1980 there was a district assembly in the San Diego Sports Arena. Leonard's assignment was to arrange hotel booking for all the out-of-town delegates. So, unlike at most assemblies, his responsibilities were done when the meetings started. As we went to the opening session we saw some people—apparently former Witnesses—picketing in front of the arena. Someone from our congregation asked what we ought to do about it. "We're not going to do anything," Leonard said. "They're on public property and they're not disturbing anyone."

Marjorie added, "It's our turn. During the thirties we used to parade in front of churches with signs like 'Religion is a snare and a racket.' " Of course this person didn't know much about our history.

What neither of us said was that we wanted to go and talk to these picketers. What information did they have?

The meeting in the Sports Arena was a bore. The message was one we had heard many times before. It was almost like a tape recording, and all the speaker had to do was lip sync. Leonard started looking around the auditorium at the people. And once again, just as in Escondido, he saw them transformed into a gray, miserable mass. He saw parents smacking their kids because they couldn't sit still. He saw them all as lifeless, without any joy or happiness or hope.

"Let's get out of here," Leonard said to Marge. On their way out of the parking lot they wrote down the phone number displayed on one of the picket signs.

Once home, we called the Los Angeles phone number and listened to a recorded message about one of the false teachings of the Jehovah's Witnesses. We felt no need to argue with what was said, for it was perfectly obvious that the message was right. An offer was given for some free literature. We wanted it, yet we wondered—what if someone found out? We could be disfellowshipped for requesting information from apostates.

We used Marjorie's middle and maiden name and hoped the mailman would deliver the parcel to our home. Two days later we received the material. The information was powerful. The writers were quoting directly from Watchtower publications to support their arguments. We looked up the quotes in our library of Society publications, and we could see for ourselves. Whoever these people were, they weren't lying.

In the packet was an opportunity to send for some books with such titles as "Apostles of Denial," "We Left Jehovah's Witnesses: A Non-prophet Organization," "Masters of Deception," and "Jehovah's Witnesses and Prophetic Speculation." We could have gone into any Christian bookstore and bought these books, but that was also forbidden. It was much too big a risk to take, so we ordered them.

What spoke to us was not so much the theological arguments but the credibility gap. The organization had misled and misinformed people and changed its mind repeatedly over the years. And it was not willing to tell us the truth now. When Leonard finished reading the last of the four books, he announced to Marjorie, "I'm resigning as an elder." He used the excuse about some family problems, since our daughter was going through a divorce. But the real reason was to spend time studying and gathering information. I believe we knew in our hearts that it was over. We stopped going to meetings and going door to door. Yet it took two more years before we were convinced. Finally, on August 24, 1982, we sent the following notarized letter to the elders of our local Kingdom Hall:

Gentlemen:

Two years ago next week, I resigned as an elder in the La Jolla Congregation, because Marjorie and I wanted to be free from the time and thought control of continuous meeting attendance, for the express reason that we had determined to make a thorough, scholarly investigation of the teachings of the Watchtower Bible and Tract Society, as they relate to the Bible.

Our heartfelt prayer to Jehovah for his guidance and direction and help in this matter continues to be answered beyond our greatest expectations. We have accumulated an extensive library, dating from the late nineteenth century to the present, and He has blessed us with a flood of information that has enabled us to come to the irrefutable conclusion that—

1) The Watchtower Bible & Tract Society is guilty of continued presumptuous prophetic speculation.
2) They have tampered with the Bible in their New World Translation, to conform to their particular teachings.
3) They have a pattern of ever-changing doctrines, 180 degrees back and forth and back again.
4) They have an enforced "unity" by an iron hand.
5) They have interjected themselves into the chain of salvation.
6) They enforce the unchristian act of shunning family members who do not agree with the Governing Body.

As you can see, we have not been hasty in our move, but have taken time to prayerfully weigh the matter and consider all the evidence.

We hereby exercise our constitutional right under the Constitution of the United States, that guarantees us freedom of choice of religion, to in fact disassociate ourselves from the Watchtower Bible and Tract Society. This letter is in accordance with the provision made in the Kingdom Ministry School Textbook, 1977 edition, pp. 61 & 62, which says, "If a baptized person insists that he wants to be no part of the congregation and he wants his name removed from all our records, we can comply with his request. If he takes such an adamant position, it would be well to encourage him to put his request in writing and it can be held in the congregation files. In a case like this the Society should be notified and a brief announcement should be made to the congregation," and later confirmed in the September 15, 1981, *Watchtower* under the subheading "Those who disassociate themselves."

By the above action, Marjorie and I have voluntarily resigned from the organization of Jehovah's Witnesses and do not recognize the Society or the Elders as having any authority over us at all. Since we have voluntarily resigned from the organization, and are therefore no longer Jehovah's Witnesses, we expressly prohibit you from disfellowshipping us or in any way defaming our character before others. If we are disfellowshipped or are slandered in any way, we will have to take legal action against you. We do not bear any personal malice against you, but we do recognize the position the Society has taken in these matters, probably due to the incredible membership losses that they are experiencing.

Rather than be disheartened at the discovery that we have been misled for over 25 years, we are filled with great joy and eager expectation of a continuing, growing, personal relationship with our loving Father and his Son, Jesus Christ.

(Signed)
Leonard Chretien
Marjorie Chretien

As soon as we mailed the letter, there was an incredible feeling of relief. No more meetings. No more Saturday service. No more disfellowshipping of people. It was over. We were free to go for a drive up the coast or sit at home and read the Sunday newspaper without feeling guilty. We were free to celebrate Christmas or visit a church if we wanted to do so. And when we visited with Christians, we found that they were not the wicked enemy we had been taught to despise.

One afternoon Marjorie, in a gesture of surrender, dropped to her knees and asked Jesus Christ to forgive her sins and come into her life. It took Leonard a little longer to see the truth about Christ. But gradually the picture opened up to him, too. This was the marvelous truth that had been hidden from us as Jehovah's Witnesses, the truth that Jesus Christ was more than just a man. He was not *a* god but *the* God come in the flesh to our planet. Through Him the marvelous plan of salvation and redemption was revealed, and today we could have a relationship with Him. We were no longer under the bondage of works, trying to knock on enough doors and attend enough meetings and obey enough rules to hopefully please Jehovah. Our destiny with Him was now sealed forever.

In the remainder of this book we want to review just a few of the areas we studied during the time we were evaluating the Witnesses. We believe you will see with us why we felt there was a huge credibility gap in the organization. You will also discover not just why we left Jehovah's Witnesses, but also how we replaced a religious organization with the Person of God Himself in our lives. Today we wouldn't dream of ever going back.

6

Chronological Deception

In 1968 Carl Olof Jonsson was a pioneer—that is, a full-time evangelist—for Jehovah's Witnesses in Sweden. One day while Jonsson was conducting a Bible study, a man challenged him to prove the date which the Watch Tower Society had chosen for the desolation of Jerusalem by the Babylonians—that is, 607 B.C. This man pointed out that historians marked that event as having occurred in either 587 or 586 B.C.

As a devoted and studious Witness, Jonsson accepted the challenge to confirm the 607 B.C. date, which is the critical link in the argument that Jesus returned invisibly to earth in 1914. His intricate research continued until the end of 1975, when Jonsson realized that the burden of evidence was against the 607 B.C. date. He developed a systematic treatise and submitted it to the Governing Body in 1977. In subsequent correspondence with the Governing Body, it became clear to Jonsson that they were unable to refute the evidence he had presented. Determined to keep their doctrinal system intact, the Watch Tower leadership warned Jonsson in a letter not to speak about his findings.

It appears that the Governing Body hoped the whole matter would either go away or that Jonsson could be intimidated into silence. In a subsequent letter to Jonsson, they stated:

> We are sure you appreciate that *it would not be appropriate for you to begin to state your views and conclusions on chronology that are different than those published by the Society so as to raise serious*

questions and problems among the brothers.[1]

The modus operandi of the Watch Tower Society is to attack the messenger and ignore the message. They employ a system of character assassination against anyone who dares to question their authority. Jonsson tells how this was employed against him and others:

> In the following months I and others who had questioned the Society's chronology began to be condemned privately as well as from the platforms of kingdom halls (meeting houses) and at Witness assemblies or conventions. We were publicly defamed and characterized in the most negative terms.... Privately, some of our Witness brothers, including a number of the Watchtower Society's travelling representatives, also intimated that we were "demon-possessed."...[2]

Ultimately, Jonsson challenged a Governing Body member to explain why attention was diverted from the question raised—the validity of the 607 B.C. date—and directed against the person who raised it. He never received an answer to his question. Instead, in July 1982, after more than 25 years as a Jehovah's Witness, he was excommunicated by a Swedish Jehovah's Witness judicial committee. According to the Swedish press, that body's members could not even read his manuscript, which had been written in English.[3]

How could such an action be possible in a supposedly Christian organization? Perhaps the answer is found in the psychological defense mechanism described by Dr. H. Dale Baumbach:

> Insecure individuals, when faced with a problem which highlights their insecurity, instinctively respond by attempting to destroy that which addresses their insecurity or to banish it to the recesses of the mind.[4]

Gentile Times

The Watch Tower Society's authority hinges on the theory that the Gentile times mentioned by Jesus in Luke 21:24 began in 607 B.C. and ended in the fall of 1914 A.D. (Russell and Nelson Barbour originally used 606 B.C., but it was quietly changed many years later because 2520 years from that date is actually 1915, not 1914.) It is argued that in 607 B.C., when Nebuchadnezzar of Babylon destroyed Jerusalem, God's visible rulership (through the nation of Israel) on the earth ended. It would not be restored until the seven Gentile times of 2520 years would pass and Christ would begin to rule invisibly as King of God's heavenly government in 1914. According to Watch Tower theology, Jesus would then cleanse the "spiritual temple" in 1918 and appoint a "faithful and discreet slave" in 1919 to serve as the representative of His heavenly government.

It becomes obvious when we back into the concept that the 1919 appointment is based on the 1918 cleansing or judgment of the "anointed class," which in turn is based upon Jesus' invisible presence and the establishing of God's heavenly government in 1914. These three dates all hinge upon the key date of 607 B.C. We cannot stress enough the importance of this linchpin date of 607 B.C. in the Watch Tower scheme of things. If 607 B.C. is wrong, then so is 1914, 1918, and of course, the 1919 "appointment."

Carl Olof Jonsson finally published his findings about the 607 date in an outstanding book entitled *The Gentile Times Reconsidered*. Jonsson's scholarly treatise goes into great detail to show the origins of the concept and argues successfully that sometimes predicted dates and important historical events accidently coincide, giving a certain credence to the predictions:

> . . . an endless number of dates have been set for the second coming of Christ, and also the end of the

Gentile times. A predicted date sometimes accidentally happens to coincide with some important historical event, although the event itself was not predicted.[5]

For example, the assassination of Archduke Francis Ferdinand
in 1914 in Sarajevo, Yugoslavia, which ignited the First World
War, was conveniently used by Charles Taze Russell to support
his prophetic teachings. He declared that the war was clearly
prophesied in Scripture, that there would be no victors, and that
the war would lead to all nations being impoverished and destroyed by Armageddon.

The modern Watch Tower would like its followers to believe
that Russell and his followers had insight from God concerning
the events of 1914. In fact, as we have seen, Russell's ideas were
not original. And when 1914 did not mark the end of the world,
the Society originated a new argument—namely, that Christ's
presence began that year, and that the generation living then
would not pass away until Armageddon occurred and the new
world system was ushered in.

The argumentation necessary to debunk the 607 B.C. date is
beyond the scope and space allowed in this work. However, Carl
Olof Jonsson establishes beyond any reasonable doubt that the
so-called Bible chronology used by the Watch Tower is false. On
the basis of ancient history, astronomy, archeology, and the Bible
itself, he presents seven separate lines of evidence which show
conclusively that Jerusalem fell to Nebuchadnezzar of Babylon in
587 B.C. rather than in 607 B.C., thus undercutting the Watch
Tower's whole system of authority.

"Undiscovered Material"

The leaders of the Watch Tower Society recognize the weak-
ness of their position. That is one reason they go to such great
lengths to defend it. Prior to becoming a member of the Governing Body, Raymond Franz, along with four other men, were

given the assignment of developing a Bible dictionary entitled *Aid to Bible Understanding*. This reference work took five years to complete. The first edition was released in 1969 and to this day remains an important reference work in the Watch Tower movement. One of the article assignments given to Franz concerned chronology, a subject that would cover some 26 pages and is the longest and most in-depth subject in the book. We will quote directly from Raymond Franz's book *Crisis of Conscience* to see what he discovered as the subject was researched. (The Watch Tower uses B.C.E.—Before the Common Era—for B.C. and C.E.—Common Era—for A.D.)

> Much of the time was spent endeavoring to find some proof, some backing in history, for the 607 B.C.E. date so crucial to our calculations for 1914. . . . We found absolutely nothing in support of 607 B.C.E.
> . . . Everything pointed to a period twenty years shorter than our published chronology claimed. Though I found this disquieting, I wanted to believe that our chronology was right in spite of all the contrary evidence. Thus, in preparing the material for the *Aid* book, much of the time and space was spent in trying to weaken the credibility of the archeological and historical evidence that would make erroneous our 607 B.C.E. date and give a different starting point for our calculations and therefore an ending date different from 1914.[6]

Despite overwhelming evidence to the contrary, Watch Tower leadership continues to stress that their chronology is "the most accurate Bible chronology available." In the Watch Tower publication *Let Your Kingdom Come* there is an appendix to Chapter 14 which is devoted to affirming the 607-1914 deception. The average Jehovah's Witness reading the appendix would be comforted by the skillful half-truths presented. Facts are deliberately concealed concerning Neo-Babylonian history. And if that were not enough, the Society states on page 187, "Even if the discovered evidence is accurate, it might be misinterpreted by modern scholars or be incomplete so that yet undiscovered material could drastically alter the chronology of the period."

Jonsson, commenting on this amazing statement, states:

> Evidently the Watchtower Society realizes that all the evidence discovered hitherto since the middle of the last century unanimously points to 587 B.C.E. instead of 607 as the eighteenth year of Nebuchadnezzar. Among the thousands of discovered documents from the neo-Babylonian era they have not been able to find the slightest support for their 607 B.C.E. date—hence, the reference to "*yet undiscovered material.*" A chronology that has to be based on "*yet undiscovered* material," because it is demolished by the *discovered* material, is resting on a weak foundation indeed. If an idea, refuted by an overwhelming mass of *discovered* evidence, is to be retained because it is hoped that "yet undiscovered material" will support it, *all* ideas, however false, could be retained on the same principle.[7]

The whole concept of the so-called "Gentile times" or 2520-year "seven times" is clearly nonsensical, and it is abundantly clear to a mind unfettered by sectarian dogmatism that the 607, 1914, 1918, and 1919 dates are hyperbolic fantasy. Nevertheless, this untenable chronology is the basis of belief for millions of Jehovah's Witnesses.

Even more incredible is the Society's teaching about the generation of 1914.

The Generation of 1914

While sitting on the Mount of Olives, Jesus' disciples asked Him about future events surrounding the destruction of Jerusalem and the end of the Jewish system, as well as His second coming. His answers were quite detailed and included a number of parables as recorded in Matthew 24 and 25. While some of Jesus' expressions had reference to events that were to unfold within a few decades, they also contained matters that would be of long-term eschatological significance. He foretold the coming destruction of Jerusalem and its magnificent temple as well as the end of the Jewish age or system. He cautioned in Matthew 24:34, "Truly I say to you, this generation will not pass away until all these things take place." And so it was. The generation living at the time Jesus spoke these words saw Jerusalem destroyed in 70 A.D. by the Romans.

The Watch Tower believes that Jesus took up kingdom power and returned invisibly in 1914, when the world entered its time of the end. This began a time period similar to the end of the Jewish age that Jesus was speaking about in the first century. The Watch Tower Society teaches that the generation of persons old enough to see and understand the events of 1914 would not pass away until the end of the age or consummation of the system of things. This belief is used to support and substantiate the whole 1914 scheme. In other words, if 1914 is indeed all that they claim it to be, then it follows that the world must end within "this generation." The question then becomes: If the generation has run out, does it follow that 1914 and all of the attendant teachings are false?

The answer to this question will become apparent as we examine Witness teaching on this subject. In order to be consistent it is necessary to use the Watch Tower Society's definition of a generation and also what they themselves have said concerning the 1914 generation.

In their Bible dictionary, *Aid to Bible Understanding*, on page 641, they define a typical generation:

> ...today much as it was in the time of Moses, people living under favorable conditions may reach seventy or eighty years of age. Moses wrote: "In themselves the days of our years are seventy years; and if

because of special mightiness they are eighty years, yet their insistence is on trouble or hurtful things; for it must quickly pass by, and away we fly." (Ps. 90:10) However, some few may live longer, but Moses stated the general rule.

The Society makes it very clear that the "generation" is not to be understood in a symbolic way but literally. They argue that Jesus was not using the term in a symbolic manner.

The "generation" of Matthew 24:34 includes persons alive at the time that the war in heaven began in 1914. All who were living or who came on the scene around that time are part of that generation. Members of that generation will see the end of the world.[8]

It is taught that persons who saw the beginning of events in 1914 will see the conclusion as well:

According to Jesus' words, at least a representative number, and perhaps many, of the generation living when his great prophecy began to be fulfilled in 1914 will see "all these things happen," including the destruction of false religion and the political systems of this world, with all their friends and supporters. . . .[9]

When the above statement was made in 1966, the Watch Tower was pushing 1975 as their latest prediction for the end of the world. The "generation" concept worked hand in glove to support the 1975 speculation, for they would witness Armageddon.

Generation . . . Going, Going, Gone

In another article, written in *Awake* in 1966, it was noted that the *youngest* of "the generation of 1914" was well over 60 years of age! In fact, the greater part of this adult generation had "already passed away in death." Based on that fact, the article concluded:

> The time left, then, is definitely limited, and it is very short. Note, too, that Jesus pointedly said "this generation *will by no means* pass away until all these things occur." So we should not look for the passing away of all members of that generation. The end of this wicked system of things will come before all members could pass away.[10]

The next few years were like a countdown. Again and again Society publications reminded readers about the generation of 1914. In 1968 the Watch Tower was stating that the "generation" was approximately 70 years old and that the youngest member of the 1914 generation would have been around 15 years of age in 1914. Clearly they were stating that the "generation" was born at the turn of the century.[11]

Three years later, in 1971, the following confident statement was printed:

> The generation living in 1914 when "these things started to occur" has now grown old. In the more than half a century that has passed, that generation's numbers have considerably diminished. Yet the "all things" foretold by Jesus for our day must occur fully before "this generation passes completely away." That means that the due time for their full occurrence must be near at hand, very close.[12]

Even when the world did not end in 1975, the Society continued to stress their adamant position as to just who the "generation" referred to. In 1978 it was stated:

> Thus when it comes to the application in our time, the "generation" logically would not apply to babies

born during World War I. It applies to Christ's followers and others who were able to observe that war and the other things that have occurred in fulfillment of Jesus' composite "sign." Some of such persons "will by no means pass away until" all of what Christ prophesied occurs, including the end of the present wicked system.[13]

Well . . . Maybe?

After 1978 the Society began to hedge. By their definition, most of the 1914 generation was 80 years old or more. They needed a more elastic definition. In a remarkable chameleonlike announcement in October of 1980, they noted that *U.S. News & World Report* assumed that ten is the age at which an event creates a lasting impression on a person's memory, and this meant that there were some 13 million Americans still alive who had a recollection of World War I. The Society article went on to note that even if the world survived to the year 2000, there would still be survivors of the World War I generation.[14]

To further their argument, they noted a review of the book *The Generation of 1914* by Robert Wohl in *The Economist* magazine:

It made this significant remark: "Eventually Mr. Wohl voices his own opinions about the generation of 1914. In a terse and condensed last chapter he suggests that generations are not mathematically definable in terms of numbers of years, but cluster around major historical crises, of which the first world war is the supreme example."—This lines up very well with the Scriptural viewpoint that Jehovah's Witnesses take on the "generation of 1914."[15]

Although we agree with Mr. Wohl that it is difficult to mathematically define generations, for the Watch Tower Society to state that this is also their viewpoint is a vain attempt to gain a few more years. The fact is that they believed and taught that the generation was at an age of understanding in 1914 and would have been born at the turn of the century.

If we use the scriptural definition of a generation in Psalm 90:10 which the Watch Tower Society uses—"As for the days of our life, they contain seventy years, or if due to strength, eighty years"—this would allow for a maximum age of 80 by reason of personal strength and good health. While there are always exceptions—some persons live beyond 80—the Society has always stressed that "the generation" would *by no means* pass away, indicating a flourishing generation and not one that has become seriously diminished. Therefore, if we use 80 years of age as the outside limit of the generation, and if we use the Watch Tower Society's benchmark of the generation having been born at the turn of the century, we must conclude that their self-imposed 1914 generation had all but passed away by 1980! Yet in *The Watchtower* of October 15, 1980 (cited above), they state that even if the world survived until the turn of the century, there would still be survivors of the World War I generation. Using their own point of reference, they are asking us to believe that persons 100 years of age be considered a generation that will have *by no means* passed away!

Sputnik

It is said that when a person is drowning, he will grasp for anything within reach in a vain attempt to hold himself up. The Governing Body, in a vain attempt to bolster or hold onto this last prophecy, have contemplated changes that only the desperate would consider. In his book, Ray Franz reveals that on February 17, 1980, three members of the Governing Body presented a document to the other members for consideration. It suggested that "this generation" should not apply to people living in 1914, but instead to the year 1957!

Why 1957? Because that was the year when the first Russian Sputnik was launched into space! These three men felt that this was the beginning of the celestial phenomenon that was the start of the fulfillment of Jesus' words at Matthew 24:29: ". . . the sun will be darkened, and the moon will not give its light, and the stars will fall from the sky, and the powers of the heavens will be shaken." They concluded their explanation by stating: "Then 'this generation' would refer to contemporary mankind living as knowledgeable ones from 1957 onward." They were not suggesting that the pivotal year of 1914 be dropped. It would remain as the "end of the Gentile times" and the enthronement of Jesus Christ. However, "this generation" would not begin until 1957![16]

If the rest of the Governing Body had bought the idea, then we guarantee it would have been introduced as "new light." It must have been very tempting, because they would have gained 43 more years. However, they did not. Nevertheless, we must not ignore the fact that three members of the Governing Body even suggested it! If anyone but a member of the Governing Body had made such a preposterous suggestion, he immediately would have been disfellowshipped.

The fact of the matter is that the "generation of 1914" doctrine is still in place, and every Jehovah's Witness alive must accept it. For those who have doubts about it, and speak about those doubts to other people, a judicial committee of elders will disfellowship them on the charge of apostasy. In the meantime, we don't know whether the Governing Body has considered any other fanciful or bizarre means to stretch the 1914 generation. However, they must realize that the "generation" is over and they will no doubt introduce "new light" on the subject.

Recently it has become apparent that such a change is in the wind. The Watch Tower organization has a practice of simply not mentioning a certain teaching for a time, so that when a change is made the passage of time buffers the impact. Until recently the following statement was printed on the inside front cover of their magazine *Awake*:

> . . . this magazine builds confidence in the creator's promise of a peaceful and secure new system before the generation that saw the events of 1914 passes away.

As of the January 8, 1987, issue, with no explanation, this statement has been removed. As this book goes to press, the Watch Tower organization has put the statement back in the May 8, 1988, *Awake*, no doubt because of mounting criticism.

Will we also see a dwindling of articles concerning the 1914 generation? Will we see a gradual buildup of articles leading in another direction? The Watch Tower Society could change the 607 B.C. date to the historically correct 587 B.C. date, thus moving 1914 to 1934. They might perhaps attempt to spiritualize the whole concept, though that would require considerable scriptural gymnastics and very persuasive argumentation on their part.

Perhaps the Society will merely stonewall the whole issue for the present and let the concept gradually diminish in the minds of the faithful. Only the future will tell how they will do it, but change they must and change they will concerning the generation of 1914.

7

Big Mother

One of the most significant moments in the life of a Jehovah's Witness is his baptism. Most Witnesses are baptized during a circuit assembly or the huge district assemblies held in giant stadiums. One after another they are led into a swimming pool to cement the most important decision of their lives.

Christians are baptized in the name of the Father, the Son, and the Holy Spirit. The formula for Jehovah's Witnesses is quite different. The person desiring to become baptized as one of Jehovah's Witnesses must answer two questions before undergoing baptism. The first question is:

> On the basis of the sacrifice of Jesus Christ, have you repented of your sins and dedicated yourself to Jehovah to do his will?

The second question is:

> Do you understand that your dedication and baptism identify you as one of Jehovah's Witnesses in association with God's spirit-directed organization?

Based on an affirmative answer to those two questions, a believer is then dipped into the water.

After his baptism, the new Jehovah's Witness is committed to slaving for the "spirit-directed organization" until his death or Armageddon, whichever comes first. For generations of

78279

Witnesses the former has been the case.

The Watch Tower Bible and Tract Society is one of the most authoritarian religious organizations in the world today. It maintains absolute control over its membership, not only in areas of religious doctrine and teaching, but also in almost every other aspect in their lives. This authority stems from the fact that it has persuaded its membership that it, and it alone, is being used by God as His earthly representative. It is claimed that God's theocratic organization has been established and made manifest here on earth, particularly since 1919, when Jesus Christ examined and selected a "faithful and discreet slave" class.

Once the modern Witness accepts the idea that Jesus chose a "slave class" to administer his affairs, it is easy to convince him that this "slave class" has a Governing Body to direct or administer the outworkings of God's visible earthly organization.

Channeling

Every dictate, change, rule, and prophetic or theological speculation comes to the individual Witness from the top down—theocratically, so to speak! It is very difficult for mortal man to argue with God. Witnesses are counseled not to use their own reasoning but to rely on Jehovah's organization, his "channel of communication":

> Theocratic ones will appreciate the Lord's visible organization and not be so foolish as to pit against Jehovah's channel their own human reasoning and sentiment and personal feelings.[1]

In the same article just quoted, *The Watchtower* magazine reminds its readers of the source of the spiritual food and the necessity that they swallow all that is presented to them without complaining:

> Are we assigned as individuals to bring forth the food for the spiritual table? No? Then let us not try to

Big Mother / 103

take over the slave's duties. We should eat and digest
and assimilate what is set before us, without shying
away from parts of the food because it may not suit the
fancy of our mental taste. The truths we are to publish
are the ones provided through the discreet-slave organization, not some personal opinions contrary to what
the slave has provided as timely food.[2]

The Watch Tower Society refers to itself as "the mother organization," even using Scriptures that only have application to a
person's physical mother to cement their authority. For example,
they use Proverbs 6:20—"Forsake not the law of thy mother"
(KJV)—as proof of their authority.[3] Further, the Society likens
the normal father-and-mother care and guidance of children to
that of God the Father and their "motherly" organization. This
emotionally conditions the Witness and engenders a strong,
almost familial loyalty to the organization. It also keeps the adult
Witness in a childlike state of dependence, always looking to
"mother" for instruction.

In an article in *The Watchtower* magazine entitled "Show
Respect for Jehovah's Organization," they contrast Christendom's "children" with the New World Society of Jehovah's
Witness "children." The "children," of course, refer to the
followers of the respective organizations. Why do Witness "children" have light while Christendom's do not? After all, both have
the same lamp—the Bible. The answer: Witnesses have accepted
enlightening instruction through the heavenly Father's motherly
organization.[4]

The article goes on to inform the Witnesses that the "mother
organization" is used by God to interpret the "light" contained
in the Bible:

The world is full of Bibles, which Book contains the
commandments of God. Why, then, do the people not
know which way to go? Because they do not also have
the teaching or law of the mother, which is light.

> Jehovah God has provided his holy written Word for
> all mankind and it contains all the information that is
> needed for men in taking a course leading to life. But
> God has not arranged for that Word to speak indepen-
> dently or to shine forth life-giving truths by itself. . . .
> It is through his organization that God provides this
> light that the proverb says is the teaching or law of the
> mother. If we are to walk in the light of truth we must
> recognize not only Jehovah God as our Father but his
> organization as our mother.[5]

Jehovah's Witnesses are taught that they alone have an exclusive understanding of God's purposes, and that all other persons
calling themselves Christian are in the dark. This includes individual Witnesses who may develop independent thinking and
endeavor to develop a personal relationship with their Creator,
thereby forsaking, as it were, "mother."

> Some who call themselves Christians and who
> claim God as their Father boast that they walk with
> God alone, that he directs their steps personally. Such
> persons not only forsake the teaching or law of the
> mother, but they literally throw God's woman out into
> the streets. The light of God's truth is not for them.[6]

That is why Witnesses are reminded, when going door to door,
to refuse any literature which a householder may offer. They are
not going to people's doors searching for truth; rather, they have
already learned the truth. So it is considered a waste of valuable
time to expose themselves to any literature other than that published by the organization.

The Witness is conditioned to believe that to resist any new
teaching or understanding that may be presented to them in the
Watch Tower literature is akin to going against God Himself. This
is done with phrases such as "Not one of Jehovah's witnesses
would deliberately insult either our heavenly Father or his motherly organization, would he?"[7] Rather, they should appreciate

the good food served by their mother, and have nothing but praise for such worthy parents.

Sometimes it is difficult for Witnesses to distinguish between their human and organizational mothers when they hear the word "mother" spoken or see it written. Indeed, besides the physical mother that every Witness has, plus the earthly, spirit-directed organization, they are taught that the woman described in Revelation 12 is a heavenly mother organization. If this seems confusing, we will later see that the Watch Tower organization also teaches that besides their natural father, the Witness has *two* heavenly Fathers, one of which is their *Grandfather*!

Be Organization-Minded

Most assuredly, the Watch Tower organization sets itself in a lofty place. Once Witnesses accept the concept that all truth comes through the "faithful and discreet slave," they hand their minds over to the mother organization to do their thinking for them, and they accept whatever is presented as coming from God. They are told, "It is vital that we appreciate this fact and respond to the directions of the 'slave' as we would to the voice of God, because it is His provision."[8]

This "voice of God" says that if Witnesses desire blessings from God they should accept the leadership of the organization, abandoning their own standards and judgment:

> Recognizing the rich blessings that Jehovah has poured out upon the "faithful and discreet slave" as a class, can we not conclude that these same benefits will result to individuals who follow that example, who pattern their course after the one taken by his organization? Why, then, should we insist on choosing our own way, setting our own standards or endeavor to evalutate our own individual judgment more highly than that of this proved faithful "slave"?[9]

This submission to the organization is especially true as it relates to finding understanding of the Bible:

Thus the Bible is an organizational book and belongs to the Christian congregation as an organization, not to individuals, regardless of how sincerely they may believe that they can interpret the Bible. For this reason the Bible cannot be properly understood without Jehovah's visible organization in mind.[10]

Thought Control

In 1978 Flo Conway and Jim Siegelman authored a book entitled *Snapping* in which they examined and documented what they term "America's epidemic of sudden personality change." They examine the changes that individuals make when abandoning the larger world community to immerse themselves in authoritarian cult religions or extravagant psychological fantasies. Conway and Siegelman state: "In America today, aware, intelligent individuals of all ages are being persuaded to stop thinking voluntarily. While many do so in their escape from the real world through authoritarian cult religions. . . ."[11] Many persons would call this process brainwashing or thought-control. Conway and Siegelman call it "information disease," which they define as an "alteration through experience of a person's fundamental information-processing capacities."

Have Jehovah's Witnesses been persuaded to stop thinking voluntarily? In a *Watchtower* article entitled "Exploring the Devil's Subtle Designs," under the subheading *Avoid Independent Thinking*, they are told that questioning the organization imitates Satan's rebellion against God:

From the very outset of his rebellion Satan called into question God's way of doing things. He promoted independent thinking. . . . How is such independent thinking manifested? A common way is by questioning the counsel that is provided by God's visible organization.[12]

In a backup article from the same issue of the *Watchtower*, there was further warning about the danger of independent thinking:

> ... there are some who point out that the organization has had to make adjustments before, and so they argue: "This shows that we have to make up our own mind on what to believe." This is independent thinking. Why is it so dangerous? Such thinking is evidence of pride. ... If we get to thinking that we know better than the organization, we should ask ourselves: "Where did we learn Bible truth in the first place? Would we know the way of the truth if it had not been for guidance from the organization? Really, can we get along without the direction of God's organization?" No, we cannot![13]

Although it may seem difficult to believe, millions of Witnesses have submitted themselves to the autocratic control of the organization. Thought-control or brainwashing connotes a negative experience. The average Witness would resist strenuously the idea that he is thus manipulated in this way. Nevertheless, millions of persons have surrendered their freedom to think for themselves, and instead they accept anything their leadership tells them.

Witnesses are instructed that they must remain loyal to the organization. The interests of the organization must be put ahead of one's own interests, or for that matter even the interests of family. To reject the organization—even for loyalty to a family member—is to reject God!

> Sometime in the future a test may be imposed upon us to comply with certain information that God brings to our attention. It may hit something that we love very dearly. What will we do? Will we hesitate in applying counsel, perhaps pondering in our mind as to what *we*

want to do about it? If that would be the case, wouldn't we really be asking ourselves the question, "Do *we* really want the rulership of God?" Would not a failure to respond to direction from God through his organization really indicate a rejection of divine rulership?[14]

Doctrinal Changes

If there is anything constant in the Watch Tower organization, it is change. The man-made theology is continually adjusted to accommodate failed prophecies or to present "new light." When "God's channel" makes prophetic blunders or changes long-held doctrines, it is difficult not to notice such events. Frequently these changes are complete turnarounds and not just minor adjustments. Naturally this creates questions in the minds of the followers. To put these issues to rest, the organization often persuades by contrived illustrations. The quotation cited below is a marvelous example of Watch Tower sleight of hand:

> At times explanations given by Jehovah's visible organization have shown adjustments, seemingly to previous points of view. But this has not actually been the case. This might be compared to what is known in navigational circles as "tacking." By maneuvering the sails the sailors can cause a ship to go from right to left, back and forth, but all the time making progress toward their destination in spite of contrary winds.[15]

Doctrinally the Watch Tower Society is more like a ship without a rudder, being tossed about by waves. Christians are counseled, "As a result, we are no longer to be children, tossed here and there by waves, and carried about by every wind of doctrine, by the trickery of men, by craftiness in deceitful scheming" (Ephesians 4:14).

Biblical Christianity, whose God is the Author of the Holy Bible, has no need to "tack" with scriptural truth. Truth is absolutely unchanging from everlasting to everlasting, and needs no excuses or bizarre illustrations to accommodate it. "The sum of Thy word is truth, and every one of Thy righteous ordinances is everlasting," writes the psalmist (Psalm 119:160). Those who must accept changed "truth" must likewise accept the lie posing as "new light."

Down through the years the organization has often reversed itself, teaching the very opposite of its former position. Because Witnesses are conditioned to expect "new light," the vast majority of Witnesses do an about-face and accept the change as a revelation from God through His channel.

Paradise Delayed

Big mother is alive and well and living in Brooklyn, New York! Her "children" live with the constant reminder of that fact. While the Christian is taught to have faith in Jesus Christ, Jehovah's Witnesses are told to put faith in an organization. An individual Witness has no direct personal relationship with the Lord Jesus Christ. Their hope of eternal life depends not upon Jesus alone but upon a chain of salvation in which the organization is an essential link. That chain consists of: a) the individual Jehovah's Witness who seeks life; b) the spirit-directed organization referred to as the "ark of salvation" or "the place of safety"; c) Jesus Christ, the Mediator; and finally d) Jehovah, the Life-giver.

This key role of the organization cannot be ignored. Should a Jehovah's Witness be disfellowshipped for any one of a number of reasons, or should a Witness disassociate himself or resign from the organization, he is taught that his relationship with God is severed. A Witness who dies either naturally or at the battle of Armageddon without reconciliation with the organization goes immediately into eternal death, along with all mankind who do not come to God's true spirit-directed organization.

The Watch Tower organization claims for itself the distinction of being the "faithful slave" who since 1919 has full authority to serve spiritual food. Under this unique authority, the organization is used as a "prophet" to prophecy future events. All persons must come to that organization for salvation and remain in good standing in order to be saved.

For over a hundred years Witnesses have been taught that the times are urgent and that it is incumbent upon them to spread the message of hope/doom. Numerous dates have been set for the end of the world, including the end-stop of the "generation of 1914." Although we are now deep into the 1980's, the message remains the same for the current crop of Witnesses. The Utopian-paradise "carrot," which is now over one hundred years old, is held before the loyal Witness, who soldiers forward with the message by selling literature and converting new victims. That "carrot" is well defined for the Witness:

> God's original purpose for humans was endless life in a Paradise *on earth*, and God's purpose cannot fail or be thwarted. . . . So can we not look forward to that endless life being enjoyed right here on planet Earth, with the earth then restored to a paradisaic condition? There are numerous proofs in the Bible that this is the proper view, that God's will will yet "take place, as in heaven also upon *earth*."[16]

Generations of Witnesses have bought the story that "millions now living will never die." Rather, they will survive Armageddon and pass into the new world, never to experience death! Almost all of the persons who heard these fanciful words when they were first spoken in 1918 are moldering in their graves, as are the "Bible Students" before them who listened to Charles Taze Russell.

Of course, the idea of a Utopian society is not new. The vision of a world wherein peace, security, and the betterment of man prevails is not exclusive to Watch Tower thinking. However, the Watch Tower organization has elevated the concept to new heights, exceeding even the wildest speculations of previous centuries. They have now added a new dimension to the Utopian concept. Witnesses not only have the earthly paradise to look forward to, but they are told that they are presently enjoying a "spiritual paradise" within the ranks of the New World Society of Jehovah's Witnesses! According to Watch Tower rhetoric, future benefits are already being enjoyed by the inhabitants of this "spiritual paradise."

In recent years the "spiritual paradise" concept has been emphasized, no doubt because the earthly paradise has stubbornly refused to arrive. An article in *The Watchtower* of October 1, 1983, entitled "Can You Enjoy Paradise Now?" had this to say on page 4:

> A PARADISE exists on earth today. It is extending farther and farther and is being enjoyed by millions of people. You, too, can be a part of it. Is this some idealistic dream? Not at all, for we are not speaking about a natural, earthly paradise but a spiritual one. . . . "What do you mean by a *spiritual* paradise?" you ask. Put simply: An organization of Christians who have made over their personalities to conform to God's requirements and who are united in his true worship may be said to be in a spiritual paradise.

The article concludes by giving examples of individuals who were formerly violent and "wolflike" and who became "lamblike" Witnesses.

Witnesses are taught that their increases in membership and their unity is in itself a fulfillment of prophecy. This is part of the spiritual paradise which must come before the literal, earthly paradise. If the New World Society of Jehovah's Witnesses exists in a spiritual paradise, the evidence in support of such a paradise should be overwhelming. What are the facts?

Today there is a virtual blizzard of material exposing the Watch Tower organization for what it really is. The Witness is particularly warned not to read this literature, because the leadership knows full well that the information contained therein is irrefutable. Much of the literature is by former Jehovah's Witnesses. Rather than address the issues they raise, the Society simply labels the writers as apostates who should be shunned.[17]

So it is that millions of Witnesses exist in a tightly sealed, closed society. A society that keeps them in constant check, not permitting the membership to examine any material that would expose the organization. A society that does all the thinking for Jehovah's Witnesses.

It sounds remarkably like another society depicted in a popular novel earlier this century. A comparison of the two is most educational. Let's see if we can find this paradise that the Watch Tower Society so desperately wants its followers to believe exists within their organization.

8

Jehovah's Happy Organization

A major publishing event occurred in 1949 when George Orwell's *1984* was released. The novel has since become the classic examination of totalitarianism. It depicts a future "super-state" of Oceania. The inhabitants of Oceania are split into three castes: a small group of powerful and brutal rulers, a larger group of middle-level bureaucrats and functionaries, and a large major-ity of mindless slaves. These are called (in order) the Inner Party, the Outer Party, and the Proles.

The doctrines of the Party in Oceania are enforced by the Thought Police, who watch for thoughtcrime, facecrime, and a multitude of smaller crimes not in keeping with the Party's aims. Opposition to the Party is punishable by death. Children are taught to spy on and turn in their parents. The Party intrudes into all personal relationships and will not tolerate any unorthodox thought.

In order to insure that everyone is thinking according to the Party line, the Party carefully alters facts to suit its present situation. It abolishes and obliterates the past through the Minis-try of Truth, a large and important department at headquarters. Clerks work incessantly at altering historical records to suit the present. Reality is what the Party decides it should be, and with power over the records, the Ministry of Truth alters it daily. The actual truth has been altered and distorted beyond recognition. As written records are destroyed or altered, and as memories fade, truth becomes whatever the Party decides. The Party of Oceania relies upon this control of reality to maintain authority over the populace. The Inner Party members have become as badly deluded by their lies as the most ignorant Outer Party members, while the bewildered Proles know nothing, and accept everything the Party tells them.

A mythical figure, Big Brother, is the head of Oceania in name only. He represents the Party. He is God, President, and friend in the quest for victory over Oceania's foes. Big Brother becomes, in effect, the Party or organization. The Party's ideology is called Ingsoc, in which control of thought and action is the essence. The credo is "Who controls the past, controls the future: who controls the present controls the past."[1]

Big Mother/Big Brother

Jehovah's Witnesses have an expression, "the truth," which refers to their religion in total. For example, a Witness might say concerning someone who has left the Watch Tower organization, "He is no longer in the truth," or perhaps about someone who is very zealous in the organization, "She really works hard for the truth." When meeting someone for the first time, a common question is, "How long have you been in the truth?" The expression originated in the days of C.T. Russell and J.F. Rutherford, when the expression used was "present truth." It has evolved into just "the truth" and has become an everyday word among Jehovah's Witnesses. Witnesses equate "truth" with the religious system of the Watch Tower organization. They believe that they alone have the truth and that all other religions are untruth according to the Watch Tower organization.

Orwell stated:

> Whatever the Party holds to be truth *is* truth. It is impossible to see reality except by looking through the eyes of the Party.[2]

That the truth changes, and changes regularly, is a given fact accepted by Society membership. The expression "present truth" as used in Russell and Rutherford's day is in reality a more accurate expression, because "present truth" is just that—for the present only. It may or may not resemble past "truth" and will become a different "truth" in the future.

Truth, as understood by Jehovah's Witnesses, changes continually as "new light shines forth." They are conditioned to expect and accept change as a normal consequence of advancing or progressive truth. Witnesses accept this phenomenon even though the change may reverse a belief long held dear and may be very costly to the individual Witness.

As with the Ministry of Truth in Orwell's society, the Watch Tower organization sanitizes its history and eliminates anything that discredits it. These adjustments by the "faithful slave" organization are made continually and are passed off as increasing "light" or a refinement of understanding:

> Things published were not perfect in the days of Charles Taze Russell, first president of the Watch Tower Bible and Tract Society; nor were they perfect in the days of J. F. Rutherford, the succeeding president. The increasing light on God's Word as well as the facts of history have repeatedly required that adjustments of one kind or another be made down to the very present time. But let us never forget that the motives of this "slave" were always pure, unselfish; at all times it has been well-meaning. . . . Actually, any adjustments that have been made in understanding have furnished an opportunity for those being served by this "slave" to show loyalty and love, the kind of love that Jesus said would mark his followers. . . . For those who truly love God's law there is no stumbling block.[3]

Once a Witness accepts this kind of logic, he will accept the continued adjustments and "increasing light." This is accomplished by distorting the previous teaching and either directly changing it or else by careful innuendo alluding to something entirely different.

An example of this is the complete distortion of facts in connection with the so-called appointment of the "faithful and discreet slave" in 1919. The story that the Watch Tower organization presents to its membership today is a fabrication. The actual facts are hidden. A completely different version of the events of the time are presented in a manner designed to legitimize the present claim. All of the events of the time period are carefully massaged and adjusted to imply fulfillment of Scripture and prophecy.

To buttress and support their credibility with the membership, it is necessary for the Watch Tower leaders to reinterpret or eliminate any reference to specific prophecies once they have failed. This is not a new concept, for C.T. Russell utilized the very same system. When the world did not end in 1914, and Russell and his followers were not raptured to glory, it was necessary to make changes in the *Studies in the Scriptures* textbooks. Volumes II and III in the *Studies* had much to say about the year 1914 and the chronology that supported it. The dates were changed in subsequent editions of these books. Russell made reference to these changes and with an adept sleight of hand dismissed them as trivial! To those who had sacrificed all in hopeful expectation, he went on to say:

> The present is a time of testing, we believe, to many of the Lord's people. Have we in the past been active merely because we hoped for our glorious change in A.D. 1914, or have we been active because of love and loyalty to the Lord and his message and the brethren![4]

This appeal to the followers to show love and loyalty to the Lord and His message was designed to provoke feelings of guilt in those who doubted.

Now You See It, Now You Don't

In 1930 Judge Rutherford admitted the failure of the Watch Tower's predictions for 1914:

> *The Watch Tower*, and its companion publications of the Society, for forty years emphasised the fact that 1914 would witness the establishment of God's kingdom and the complete glorification of the church. During that period of forty years God's people on earth were carrying on a witness work, which work was fore-shadowed by Elijah and John the Baptist. All of the Lord's people looked forward to 1914 with joyful expectation. When that time came and passed there was much disappointment, chagrin and mourning, and the Lord's people were greatly in reproach. They were ridiculed by the clergy and their allies in particular, and pointed to with scorn, because they had said so much about 1914, and what would come to pass, and their "prophecies" had not been fulfilled.[5]

This was a rare admission of the fact that the Watch Tower organization had made grandiose prophecies concerning 1914. In an excellent Orwellian example of the "past being controlled by the present," 55 years later the organization altered the past, presenting an entirely different view of the time period to a new generation of Jehovah's Witnesses:

> From 1876 onward, Jehovah's people served notice upon the world, and particularly upon Christendom, that the Gentile Times would end in the fall of 1914. The clergy could not ignore this preliminary work of almost 40 years—a work corresponding to that of John the Baptizer. Those clergymen waited eagerly to pounce upon this journal's editor should 1914 pass without any outstanding events to correspond with

those about which he warned. But, oh, how they were
silenced when on July 28, 1914, peace was shattered
by the outbreak of World War I![6]

They state that from 1876 onward the organization had pointed
to 1914 as the end of the Gentile Times, which is true. However,
they neglect to mention that the organization had also prophesied
that 1914 would see the end of the world and the glorification or
rapture of the church, as admitted by Rutherford. The above
quote implies that the outbreak of the first World War silenced the
clergymen, connoting that the war was what had been prophesied. Rutherford's earlier statement showed that in 1914 the
clergy had much reason to ridicule the organization. In actual fact
the war was incidental to the grandiose claims that the Watch
Tower organization had made! This example is but one of numerous expedient adjustments continually made to color the facts of
Watch Tower history.

Orwell wrote:

> And since the Party is in full control of all records,
> and in equally full control of the minds of its members,
> it follows that the past is whatever the Party chooses to
> make it.[7]

Whoops!

From time to time the Watch Tower organization changes
doctrinal positions or explanations within the course of the same
year! For example, in 1975 the book *Man's Salvation Out of
World Distress Is at Hand* stated on page 208, in connection with
the parable of the mustard grain:

> It is the fake "kingdom of the heaven," the counter-
> feit, namely, Christendom, that is filled with these
> symbolic birds, "the sons of the wicked one." Today it

is big enough to hold them all. In the parable, the "man" that sowed the mustard grain pictures the "wicked one," Satan the Devil.

Later in the same year of 1975, in the *Watchtower* of October 1, on page 600, the sower of the mustard grain changed from Satan, the Devil, to Jesus Christ! The *Kingdom Ministry* of November 1975 explained briefly:

> In the October 1, 1975, "Watchtower," page 600, paragraph 22, we read: "Jesus Christ, with his prophetic foresight, could foreknow the outcome for the symbolic mustard grain that he planted in the first century." So Jesus is to be considered as the planter referred to in this parable. An adjustment is being made in the printing of all future copies of the "Man's Salvation" book to read in harmony with this viewpoint.

Orwell wrote:

> This holds good even when, as often happens, the same event has to be altered out of recognition several times in the course of a year.[8]

The Watch Tower organization takes pride in presenting itself as keepers of integrity—people who are loyal to God and His organization, who will endure all manner of persecution for "the truth." To that end there is a continual barrage of articles designed to convey this image. The following incident reveals how the organization will alter facts to foster this image and present Witnesses in a favorable light. In the April 15, 1982, *Watchtower* article, on page 25, the following account was presented in an article entitled "Enduring Joyfully Despite Persecution":

> In March, 1963, at Gbarnga, Liberia, about 400 persons attending a district assembly of Jehovah's Witnesses were rounded up and held for four days without

food at a military compound. In an effort to force
them to compromise their religious beliefs and salute
the Liberian flag, the Witnesses were ill. treated and
their belongings were plundered. While a few did give
way and compromise because of fear, the great majority maintained integrity.

Millions of Witnesses were no doubt thrilled to read about
these faithful brothers and sisters. Since the source cited for the
information was the 1977 *Yearbook*, a number of Witnesses
decided to go and read the actual account for themselves. They
discovered that the Yearbook actually said that the majority
compromised their faith. There must have been many inquiries
about this, because in *The Watchtower* of July 15, 1982, on page
31, we read:

The Statement in the Watchtower of April 15, 1982,
is in error. Actually, according to the Yearbook of
1977, pages 176 and 178, there were about 100 Liberian Witnesses who went through the Gbarnga persecution maintaining integrity, while approximately
200 compromised their faith. . . .

The article then goes on to obliquely say that, of course, the
worldwide picture is far more encouraging—no doubt the great
majority have proved faithful under persecution. The writers of
the April 15 article "Enduring Joyfully Despite Persecution" had
to review the 1977 *Yearbook* account to be able to quote from it.
Besides bringing into question the integrity and honesty of the
writers of the article, what about the committee that approved it
for publication? A committee of members from the Governing
Body of Jehovah's Witnesses check and approve all articles before publication.

This altered incident was used to prove that Jehovah's Witnesses are faithful under test or persecution and that those who
attend meetings regularly are "the loyal ones." The facts are that

among the compromisers were seven congregation servants (presiding overseers), nine special pioneers (full-time missionaries), and one Gilead graduate! These persons, all appointed by headquarters, must certainly have been regular meeting attenders. If the Watch Tower had not been caught, this deception would have become part of the record.

Orwell states:

> The past was erased, the erasure was forgotten, the lie became truth.[9]

How can the authors of these articles write such distortions of fact? It becomes understandable after an investigation of the organization's past record of fact manipulation. As in Orwell's Ministry of Truth, it is company policy. No area is sacred. Renowned Greek scholars are misquoted. Historic and archeological facts are denied or twisted. Even the Bible itself is adjusted to fit Society theology. The book *Jehovah's Witnesses in the Divine Purpose* is a totally biased history, relating the story about the movement as the organization would have it appear, and not as it actually is. Articles in current publications use quotations from earlier publications, ostensibly to substantiate their claim of the moment. However, these quotes are interspersed with ellipses, editing out what was really said, which is often opposite to what they are trying to imply, just as in the Gbarnga, Africa story.

Orwell stated:

> Books, also, were recalled and rewritten again and again, and were invariably reissued without any admission that any alteration had been made.[10]

Should a Jehovah's Witness decide to do some research, there is a Watch Tower Index available to assist them through the labyrinth of publications. How is it then that the Witness is unaware of these deceptions? Usually the Witness is so busy that he has little time to do in-depth research. Also, the Watch Tower "Ministy of Truth" removes damaging references from newer editions of the indexes.

So we see that, as in Orwell's Ministry of Truth, the Watch Tower organization has twisted truth to fit their goals. But there is another interesting parallel between Orwell's state and Jehovah's Witnesses—the Ministry of Love.

Ministry of Love

Oceania's Ministry of Love had as its goal the total regimentation of the subjects of the Party. This was accomplished by an elaborate spy system in which everybody reported on everybody else. Any deviation from the Party line and ideology had to be reported, and those reported on were severely punished. No one was exempt. Wives reported on husbands, husbands on wives, children on parents, parents on children.

Within the congregations of Jehovah's Witnesses, all members are counseled to turn in other members should they become aware of some infraction against organizational policy. They report on each other to the congregation elders, who are equivalent to Orwell's Thought Police. Witnesses receive this counsel:

> It requires strength of Christian personality to inform appointed elders of the serious sin of a fellow believer. But if we are to have Jehovah's favor, we must not let personal friendship blind us to the wrongdoing of another individual. Our relationship with God is of far greater importance than loyalty to a friend who is guilty of serious wrongdoing and refuses to reveal the matter to the appointed elders.[11]

Parents are counseled to turn in their children or else share in the sin. Wives and husbands are not exempt and frequently turn each other in to the elders. Even elders are not exempt, and one elder may report another elder. Jehovah's Witnesses are taught that if they do not inform on each other, then they are actually sharing in the sin committed by the wrongdoer.[12]

Witnesses have a rather long list of what they may or may not do. They may not salute a flag, must not attend another church, can't celebrate birthdays, Christmas, or other traditional holidays, cannot question Watch Tower teaching, cannot serve in the military or work for a military or political organization . . . the rules go on and on. With these regulations, gleaned from Watchtower teaching, Jehovah's Witnesses become in effect the conscience of other members of the congregation. This procedure of spying and reporting on each other goes on not only at the congregation level at the local Kingdom Halls but also at the various branch offices, missionary homes, and even Brooklyn Bethel headquarters.

Paul Blizard, a former worker at Watch Tower headquarters in Brooklyn, told us that people spied on each other at headquarters and turned one another in. "I thought it was incredible that someone was watching me every moment of the day," he said.

Gary Botting, a second-generation Witness, wrote about his pioneer work in Hong Kong as a young man. At first he lived at the Bethel branch office, "where I received a curious initial assignment—spying on the two Chinese translators, both of whom were graduates of the Watch Tower Society's missionary school of Gilead.[13]

Orwell wrote:

> We have cut the links between child and parent, and between man and man, and between man and woman. No one dares trust a wife or a child or a friend any longer.[14]

Judicial Committee

What happens when a person is reported to the elders? The offender is brought before a judicial committee of elders. This committee holds the power to reprove, counsel, or disfellowship (excommunicate) according to its decision. The offender is interrogated, sometimes mercilessly, and the judicial committee decides if the offender may have somebody speak in his defense or not. Accusers may or may not be identified to the accused and their testimony usually is given to the elders without the accused being present. Although there is an appeal arrangement for those judged guilty, the original decision of the elders is rarely overturned.

When a person is disfellowshipped from the organization, he is treated like a leper. He must be totally shunned by Witnesses. He cannot even be greeted on the street. Should a Witness decide to ignore this rule and associate with the disfellowshipped friend or relative, he in turn will be disfellowshipped.

Because the Watch Tower organization is losing hundreds of thousands of its members to what it terms apostasy, and because these persons have disassociated (resigned) from the organization, the Watch Tower now includes these persons in their shunning program. This, of course, is a clever device to keep the membership ignorant as to the real reasons why these so-called apostates have left the organization.

These persons are not apostates in the biblical sense. They have not abandoned God and Christ Jesus. Rather, they have discovered the truth about the Watch Tower and have turned their back on it. This dark device of shunning is a high form of censorship, because if the leadership permitted the rank-and-file Witness to communicate with persons who have disassociated themselves, the floodgates would be opened, and they could not contain the exodus!

Many Witnesses are being held hostage by the organization because if they speak out or decide to disassociate from the organization, they will be separated from their families. They hang on because they cannot bear the thought of not seeing or having any contact with their parents, children, grandchildren, or other relatives.

The life of a disfellowshipped person can be very lonely. It is difficult to step back into the normal world. A woman living alone in a small town relates that she spends much of her time sitting in pizza parlors watching television just to fulfill her need to be around other people. This lady was disfellowshipped for playing bingo. She enjoyed the company of people at these games, and it alleviated her loneliness. The elders told her that she was disfellowshipped because bingo was a form of greed! Her Jehovah's Witness son will see her only when it is absolutely necessary, and she therefore rarely sees her grandchild.[15]

The stories of broken lives caused by the practice of disfellowshipping and shunning is heartbreaking. One woman wrote to tell us she was disfellowshipped for disagreeing with official Watchtower theology. Less than a year later, her 17-year-old daughter died of chronic asthma. Although neither the daughter nor the husband had been disfellowshipped, the family did not receive a single sympathy card from any of the hundreds of Witnesses with whom they were acquainted.

Another woman was turned into the elders by her husband. Her offense: voting in a primary election. She was quickly disfellowshipped and her husband divorced her.

An elderly man lay in the hospital, dying of cancer. The only chance he had for continued life was to accept a blood transfusion. The elders in his congregation heard about it and forced their way into his hospital room. After grilling him concerning his "sin," they disfellowshipped him. The experience was so shattering that the man died shortly thereafter.

A teenage girl committed suicide when she thought she might be disfellowshipped. Then the Witnesses in the community were told not to attend the girl's funeral. However, the overseer of the congregation and two women who defied the edict were disfellowshipped for standing with the parents of the girl during the funeral.

The examples could go on and on. We have in our files numerous heartbreaking letters and notes from phone calls we have received from all over North America. They show deep pain in the face of unbelievable callousness on the part of the organization. One of the most unfeeling cases was reported in the Wenatchee (Washington) *World* newspaper. A local woman, 85 years old, who had been a faithful witness for 43 years, was forced to choose between love for her son—who was critical of the Watchtower Society—and loyalty to the organization. She chose her son. "The worst thing is that I can't talk to any of my friends any more," she said after she was disfellowshipped.

Although the ultimate control is in the hands of the high-level leadership, the judicial committee system serves as an effective control mechanism at the congregation level. From the day a person becomes a Witness to the day he dies or leaves the movement, he is under the eye of the congregation elders who police his life.

Orwell:

> A Party member lives from birth to death under the eye of the Thought Police. Even when he is alone he can never be sure that he is alone.[16]

Once a Witness begins to think for himself and realizes that he is following a man-made dictatorial organization, he can do one of two things: He can either leave and suffer the consequences or else remain in the organization for the sake of his family relationships. Usually, however, it is just a matter of time before his true feelings and thinking become obvious.

Orwell:

> Thought-crime was not a thing that could be concealed forever. You might dodge successfully for a while, even for years, but sooner or later they were bound to get you.[17]

Rick Townsend, a former Witness elder, told us of a case where a Witness man and wife, over a period of time, came to doubt Watch Tower doctrine. The matter came to the attention of the body of elders, who were unable to answer the biblical questions this couple raised. Rick emphasized that the couple posed these questions in a very open, nonbelligerent manner, as they sincerely desired to know the truth. Finally the whole body of elders decided to phone Watch Tower headquarters to see if they might have logical answers to give to this couple. The elders were asked if the Witness couple questioned the doctrines of the Watch Tower. The elders answered in the affirmative. The service department representative said, "You don't have to answer their questions. Disfellowship them!"

Orwell wrote:

> The more the Party is powerful, the less it will be tolerant.[18]

The Watch Tower organization disfellowships over a hundred persons a day, which is probably some kind of record in religious circles. The following statement is from *The Watchtower* of January 1, 1986, on page 13:

> Shocking as it is, even some who have been prominent in Jehovah's organization have succumbed to immoral practices, including homosexuality, wife swapping, and child molesting. It is noted, also, that during the past year, 36,638 individuals had to be disfellowshipped from the Christian congregation, the greater number of them for practicing immorality.

Facecrime

Witnesses must at all times conduct themselves in a manner that shows complete and utter respect for those in authority. This has particular application to the women in the organization. At a circuit assembly in a talk entitled "Theocratic Subjection," Witness women were told, "Sisters should not express disagreement with judicial decisions of the elders *even by their facial expressions.*" Joan Cetnar was a fourth-generation Jehovah's Witness who worked at Brooklyn Bethel headquarters. She relates:

> One day I was notified to report to Brother Larson at the factory to accept a new duty there. He informed me I would have a desk in the Correspondence Department. I would be responsible for opening mail from one section of the country and dispersing it to the proper departments in the factory. . . . I was very pleased to be able to serve Jehovah in this (I thought) responsible position. So when, after several months, I was told to report downstairs to the Magazine Department to work, I was crushed, for I considered this a demotion. I felt I had not been faithful in the assignment Jehovah had given me. Also I couldn't understand why my overseer, Brother Harley Miller, had not come to me and lovingly told me how I had proved unworthy. Because I had known Brother Larson, the factory servant, from childhood, I felt I could discuss the matter with him. He informed me that my removal was because of a facial expression I had made to Brother Miller which showed a lack of respect for him.[19]

Orwell:

> In any case, to wear an improper expression on your face (to look incredulous when a victory was announced, for example) was itself a punishable offense. There was even a word for it in Newspeak: *facecrime*, it was called.[20]

Witness lives revolve around a heavy schedule imposed by the leadership. All else is put to the side and little time is afforded for personal or family interests. Paul Blizard, in the film *Witnesses of Jehovah*, had this to say:

Even though we believed that God was love, we were always afraid that He was going to zap us, that sometime Armageddon might come and we might not make it. If we didn't go out in door to door ministry on a weekend but took our family out to the lake or something, we felt guilty all the time.

Why would Paul feel this way? Because of statements like the one in the June 1, 1985, *Watchtower* magazine, on page 12. Under a picture of a Witness father and his small daughter standing at a doorstep with literature bags in hand, the caption reads: "While fellow witnesses of Jehovah are engaging in theocratic pursuits, are you and your family often heading for some recreation spot?"

Orwell:

In principle a Party member had no spare time, and was never alone except in bed. It was assumed that when he was not working, eating, or sleeping he would be taking part in some kind of communal recreations; to do anything that suggested a taste for solitude, even to go for a walk by yourself, was always slightly dangerous. There was a word for it in Newspeak: *ownlife*, it was called, meaning individualism and eccentricity.[21]

Blind Loyalty

Watch Tower leadership holds complete and total power over the membership through the concept that the theocracy is in place. Therefore, if Witnesses desire to please God they must obey His divinely appointed "faithful slave" organization. To do otherwise would be tantamount to being disloyal to God. This loyalty to the organization and the Governing Body has reached fanatical proportions. At the large conventions of Witnesses held worldwide in 1985, a discourse was given with the title "Carefully Following the Orders of the King." During the course of the talk, which centered on loyalty to the Watch Tower organization, the following was stated: "We should be working under the direction of the Governing Body and the older men in our congregations . . . and if one of those instructions were for us to jump, our only response should be 'How high?' and 'How far?' "

Orwell:

> There will be no loyalty, except loyalty toward the Party. There will be no love, except the love of Big Brother.[22]

The degree to which this blind loyalty can lead is best illustrated by a personal experience of a few years ago. A circuit overseer, while giving a pep talk to a group of elders, said "If the society told me that wall over there was black, then I would believe it is black." The wall was white!

Orwell:

> The key word here is *blackwhite*. . . . Applied to a Party member, it means a loyal willingness to say that black is white when Party discipline demands this. But it means also the ability to *believe* that black is white, and more, to *know* that black is white, and to forget that one has ever believed the contrary.[23]

This is further illustrated with the 1975 prophecy failure. The Watch Tower denies that they prophesied the end of the world for that year. Today if you ask a Witness about 1975 he will state that the organization did not predict the end of the world. In fact, at a Witness assembly in the spring of 1985, a talk entitled "How We Know We Have The Truth" was given. During the discourse the Watch Tower spokesman raised the subject of 1975 and asked the audience, "What were we looking forward to? To survive beyond '75." After a pause he said, "Well, didn't we?" The audience responded with protracted and vigorous applause even though this was a tacit admission of the failed prophecy.

Orwell:

> The Party told you to reject the evidence of your eyes and ears. It was their final, most essential command.[24]

9

A Different Gospel

The Lord Jesus while sitting on the Mount of Olives told His disciples, "This gospel of the kingdom shall be preached in the whole world for a witness to all the nations, and then the end shall come" (Matthew 24:14).

What exactly is this gospel? The apostle Paul declared to the Corinthians, "Now I make known to you, brethren, the gospel which I preached to you" (1 Corinthians 15:1). And then, if there was any doubt about what he meant, Paul made it absolutely clear:

> I delivered to you as of first importance what I also received, that Christ died for our sins according to the Scriptures, and that He was buried, and that He was raised on the third day according to the Scriptures, and that He appeared to Cephas, then to the twelve. After that He appeared to more than five hundred brethren at one time, most of whom remain until now, but some have fallen asleep" (1 Corinthians 15:3-6).

So the gospel is the good news concerning Jesus Christ—that He lived, died for our sins, and rose again. This good news has been preached by Christians for almost 2000 years and continues to be preached in all the inhabited earth even as it was preached in the first century.

Is this the good news of the kingdom preached by Jehovah's Witnesses? If it is not, then millions of Witnesses have been put in a precarious position by their leadership. For the apostle Paul wrote, "But even though we or an angel from heaven should preach to you a gospel contrary to that which we have preached to you, let him be accursed" (Galatians 1:8).

Despite Paul's warning, Jehovah's Witnesses preach that God's kingdom was established invisibly in 1914, and therefore the gospel preached for almost 2000 years has never been the true gospel!

> Let the honest-hearted person compare the kind of preaching of the gospel of the Kingdom done by the religious systems of Christendom during the centuries with that done by Jehovah's Witnesses since the end of World War I in 1918. They are not one and the same kind. That of Jehovah's Witnesses is really "gospel," or "good news," as of God's heavenly kingdom that was established by the enthronement of his Son Jesus Christ at the end of the Gentile Times in 1914.[1]

Watch Tower leaders claim that all of the preaching done by Christendom's missionaries has been a waste of time. The real good news has been preached by Jehovah's Witnesses since 1914-1918.

> Scoffers at this may minimize this achievement and emphasize that the missionaries of Christendom during the centuries past got to all those places before ever the Christian witnesses of Jehovah came along. True! But the Kingdom witnessing of Jehovah's Witnesses since 1914 has been something far different from what Christendom's missionaries have published both before and since 1914.
>
> "Different"—how so? In that it has not been a witness concerning the kingdom mentioned in Colossians 1:13, "the kingdom of the Son of [God's] love," into which the 144,000 "sealed" spiritual Israelites

have been transferred already. What Jehovah's Witnesses have preached world wide since 1918 is something unique, something that has distinguished these as being the "last days" of the political, social, judicial, militarized system of things. It has been a worldwide witness concerning a royal government now set up in the heavens, empowered to oust the Devil and his demons from the location of its throne.[2]

When Witnesses come calling door to door, they claim that they are fulfilling Matthew 24:14, and that their proclamation of "this good news of the kingdom" is therefore a hallmark of the one true organization that God is using. This is a primary doctrine of the Watch Tower Society. They believe that their organization is the only one fulfilling this mandate.

The test of the "good news" or gospel must be this: Is it supported by the Scriptures? Does the Watch Tower's "good news" line up with that taught by the early Christians? Did Jesus or any of the apostles specify the year when God's kingdom would begin exercising its influence toward the earth? Would Jesus have associates who would have the power to cleanse persons of sin and imperfection? These are some of the issues raised by Jehovah's Witnesses.

We will examine the official teaching of the Watch Tower concerning the good news of the kingdom, using their major present teaching aid, first printed in 1968 and entitled *The Truth that leads to Eternal Life*. This book states that God's kingdom is a government and has come to power:

> Jehovah promised, however, that at the end of that time he would take direct action against all rebels and opposers of his rule. And he would bring the earth and its inhabitants completely under his rule again. How? By the Kingdom, a new heavenly government under his Son Christ Jesus. So the coming of that kingdom to power means that great changes are near at hand.[3]

In other words, Jesus Christ has already set up His rule—invisibly, as we've already noted, in 1914. Therefore we are living in the last days of the system of things. Providing persons gain Jehovah's approval, they can survive the end of the world and live into the new system under God's kingdom.[4]

This kingdom government is going to restore righteousness to the planet with no division or nationalism. People of all races and nationalities will be one family of brothers and sisters, united in pure worship of the heavenly Father.[5] Until then, it is claimed that Jesus Christ rules invisibly from the heavens with 144,000 elect persons taken from the planet. The elect is limited to 144,000 only, and they become co-rulers with Christ. No one else can gain access to heaven.[6]

The Watch Tower bases this teaching on Revelation 5:10. In its own version of the Bible, called the *New World Translation*, we read, "You made them to be a kingdom and priests to our God, and they are to rule as kings over the earth." This is an example of how the Watch Tower organization changes the Scriptures to fit their theology. All recognized translations of Holy Scripture are rendered to the effect that the kings rule *upon* the earth, not over it. For example, the New American Standard Bible reads at Revelation 5:10, "Thou hast made them to be a kingdom and priests to our God; and they will reign upon the earth." The King James Version renders the final part of the verse "We shall reign on the earth." The Living Bible renders it "They shall reign upon the earth." Today's English Version, the New International Version, Phillips Modern English, the Revised Standard Version, and The New English Bible all translate the final phrase "on" or "upon" the earth.

In 1969 the Watch Tower organization produced *The Kingdom Interlinear Translation of the Greek Scriptures*. They took the original Greek text and rendered a word-for-word translation in English underneath each line. Then in a parallel column they provided the English text, using their *New World Translation*. The translation printed directly underneath the original Greek words for Revelation 5:10 reads, "and they are reigning upon the earth." Nevertheless, the *New World Translation* printed alongside reads, "and they are to rule as kings over the earth."

The reason we have gone to such length with this example is to show that the Watch Tower organization will torture even the most obvious biblical rendering to fit their theology.

Historic biblical Christianity teaches that the glorified church or body of Christ will reign with Christ during the millennial reign. The Bible teaches a visible second advent or return of Christ to the earth, at which time the glorified church will reign there with Him (Revelation 5:10; 20:6). The bride of Christ or body of Christ is not limited to 144,000 people but rather is a "great multitude" which no one can count (Revelation 7:9).

On the other hand, Watch Tower theology states that Christ will never return visibly, but in fact has already come in an invisible presence, and that the bride of Christ is limited to 144,000 chosen ones who will rule with Him invisibly *over* rather than *upon* the earth during the millennial reign of one thousand years.

The 144,000

At this point it is necessary to elaborate somewhat on the 144,000 concept. The Watchtower Society teaches that body of Christ, those who have the hope of heaven, is limited in number to 144,000. Those believers who are not part of the 144,000 form a secondary class, known as the great crowd of "other sheep." These believers can never experience heaven, but will live on the new earth following Armageddon. They teach that the gathering of 144,000 began in the first century and continued through the year 1935.

Why 1935? The date was chosen by Judge Rutherford when he realized that the organization was growing and would take in far more than 144,000 people. The 144,000 elect theory included all Christians from Pentecost forward. Rutherford decided that the Witnesses then living, plus the early Christians, filled the quota. So his solution was to close the door to heaven and designate a secondary group who would live forever upon the earth and could grow to any number. Presto, problem solved! This, it was explained, represented the "great crowd" in Revelation 7:9-17.

Therefore, part of the good news of Jehovah's Witnesses is that only 144,000 persons are born again into the body of Christ and will inherit heavenly glory! The rest of the "other sheep" cannot be born again. They cannot share in Christ's heavenly kingdom. They cannot be completely justified through faith in Jesus Christ. They cannot experience the baptism of the Holy Spirit. And they cannot participate in the sacrament of holy communion. In other words, whereas historic Christianity has invited all who wanted to come and partake in Christ's kingdom, the Watch Tower Society deprives its followers of that hope.

Former Jehovah's Witness David Reed, in his book *Jehovah's Witnesses Answered Verse by Verse*, states concerning this issue:

> Where does the Bible teach that entrance to the Christian congregation would be closed in the year 1935, with a secondary "great crowd" being gathered after that? Nowhere! Watchtower leaders claim that "light flashed up"—that Watchtower president J. F. Rutherford received a special "revelation of divine truth"—to introduce this change in 1935. They can produce *no scriptural support at all* for the 1935 date. . . .
>
> There is no biblical basis whatsoever for this teaching. Scripture discusses in detail the Old Covenant for the Jews and the New Covenant for Christians. But it makes no mention of any third arrangement for gathering a "great crowd" with an earthly hope after the year 1935.
>
> Moreover, the verses the Witnesses cite in Revelation actually locate the "great crowd" as "before the throne of God" (7:15, NWT), and "in his temple" (7:15, NWT)—all *heavenly* locations, rather than on earth as the Watchtower Society teaches.[7]

Besides the 144,000 co-rulers with Christ, the Watch Tower organization teaches there will be visible representatives of the invisible heavenly government here on the planet:

> But will this heavenly government have any visible representatives? Yes, indeed! Why, even now the heavenly administration appoints faithful men as its representatives in the Christian congregation, doing so by means of God's holy spirit. So we can be confident that Christ will see to it that the right men on earth are assigned to represent the Kingdom government, for then he will be taking a direct hand in earth's affairs. Because these men represent the King in a special way, the Bible calls them "princes."[8]

We have already noted that vice-president Franz identified and changed the "princes'" concept in 1950. He told an international convention that the "princes" were not the ancient worthies that had been expected to be resurrected for well over 25 years, but rather the appointed servants within the Watch Tower organization. This is taught to the present day. And when the new world order is ushered in after the "world of ungodly people" is destroyed, Christ will use experienced overseers and elders as His representatives.[9]

So there we have it: Christ will rule invisibly along with 144,000 co-rulers over the earth. His visible representatives upon the earth will be none other than Jehovah's Witness elders who have passed through Armageddon. They will have oversight over the multitudes of Witnesses who have also passed through Armageddon. These Armageddon survivors have the prospect of eternal life providing they pass a final test at the end of the thousand years.

Priestly Saviors

Another aspect of the Witness good news is that a government such as the world has never seen will be in operation. This government will have a power lacking in all human govenments. The Scriptures teach that through the merit of Jesus Christ's atonement, mankind may be forgiven and cleansed of sin. However, the Watch Tower organization goes further and teaches that the 144,000 co-rulers that serve as a priesthood will have the power to cleanse persons of sin and imperfection!

> The initial program of the Kingdom will cover a period of one thousand years. During that time Jesus Christ and the members of his heavenly government will serve not only as kings but also as priests of God on behalf of all their human subjects. . . . They will have a power that has been lacking in all human governments till now: the power to cleanse persons of sin and imperfection. This power rests in God's heavenly priesthood by means of Jesus' ransom sacrifice. . . . By making continual progress in righteousness and with the help of the heavenly priesthood, they will progressively grow young and strong, until they reach perfection of health in mind and body. They will be set completely free from the bondage to sin and death inherited from Adam.[10]

Jehovah's Witnesses believe that during the millennial reign the general resurrection will take place over a period of time and the earth will be restored to paradisiacal conditions. However, their salvation is not yet assured. All Armageddon survivors, their offspring, and the resurrected ones must go through a final test at the end of the thousand years. It might be likened to salvation on the time payment plan.

> God's kingdom by Christ will rule for all eternity. However, by the close of the first thousand years it will have accomplished a particular purpose toward the earth. It will have removed every trace of unrighteousness. All humankind on earth will stand as perfect

creatures before the throne of the Supreme Judge, Jehovah God. In every respect they will be equal to the perfect humans in Eden. Will they be worthy to have God grant them the right to everlasting life? It will be proper that the Kingdom subjects be tested as to their devotion to God's righteous rule. Jehovah will give them the opportunity to show their loyalty. How? By releasing Satan and his demons from their condition of restraint in the "abyss." By this test each one in God's earthly family may individually have the privilege of giving a personal answer to the challenge made to their heavenly Father by Satan. Those who stay loyal to God will be judged worthy of everlasting life.[11]

Witnesses believe that God's kingdom is just around the corner, although this claim has now been made for well over a hundred years. It is currently taught that the "time of the end" began in 1914, when Jesus Christ was enthroned in the heavens. The generation that witnessed the events of 1914 will "by no means" pass away until God destroys the present system of things, including all persons who have not become Jehovah's Witnesses. They emphasize that the time remaining is short, for "this generation is getting up in years now."[12]

More than 20 years have passed since these statements were printed in *The Truth That Leads to Eternal Life*. This is a problem that the Watch Tower leadership has created for itself, because, as has already been shown, the generation of 1914 is gone!

Nevertheless, Witnesses believe that the world is deep into its time of the end and that they are engaged in a "separating" work. They separate themselves from the world in general, but more importantly, from all other religions. This separating work, of course, involves the door-to-door, house-to-house literature-selling and study work. In fact, Witnesses are taught that this ministry is a sacred duty and essentially the means by which they will be saved. The July 15, 1979, *Watchtower* stated on page 14,

"It is by our endurance in proclaiming 'the good news of the kingdom' that we may attain to salvation."

Faith without works is dead. That is the message of the epistle of James. Witnesses are taught that works means primarily door-to-door activity. They believe that it is necessary to teach interested persons Watch Tower dogma so they can be separated from the influence of false religion. This is accomplished by the study of a Watch Tower publication which promotes the organization as the only source of truth. It is virtually impossible for a Witness to teach a potential convert from the Bible alone, for the Witness doctrines are too complicated and many of them have no basis in fact in the Bible. So Witnesses are encouraged to spread the good news by using Society publications which are presented as spiritual food coming from God Himself.

> Knowing how much you personally have benefited from reading and studying the Society's publications, you will no doubt want to share with others the things you have learned. With the use of the Society's publications, even new ones can accomplish much good in preaching the good news from house to house.[13]

Persons interested in the Watch Tower "good news" are encouraged from the beginning of their studies to reach out and speak with relatives, friends, work associates, and others. This will ultimately result in having them share in the door-to-door literature-selling as they become more qualified. All persons are directed to what is referred to as "the ark of salvation" or protection, which is the Watch Tower organization. Those in the "ark"—that is, the Watch Tower Society—will pass safely through "the 'great tribulation' into the pollution-free earth beyond!"[14]

Part and parcel with the preaching of the Watch Tower good news is the separation or dividing of people, based on the Society message. The separation becomes a choice that people must make when presented with that message. Should they accept it, they are sheep. Should they reject it, they are classed as goats. In some parts of the world the populace have an opportunity a number of times each year to make that choice when called on by Witnesses. In other parts of the world the populace have never even heard of Jehovah's Witnesses, let alone their message.

According to the Watch Tower, the end is just around the corner. Yet they also emphasize the words of Christ stating that the gospel must be preached to the entire world. How then is it that everybody gets an opportunity to make a choice? While the sheep will pass through Armageddon, the goats will be destroyed at Armageddon. The Watch Tower leadership likes to point to the number of persons baptized as Jehovah's Witnesses each year. They argue that Jehovah held back the storm of Armageddon so that many more could be saved, while at the same time insisting that those who have not accepted their message will be doomed. The fact of the matter is that the number of persons baptized each year in comparison to those born into the world is minuscule. In other words, while perhaps 200,000 persons may come into the "ark of protection" as sheep, millions and millions of babies are born to destruction as goats. The economy of this paradox is never considered as the separating of sheep and goats goes forward.

Please notice in the following quotation the oblique mention of the three major false prophecies of 1914, 1925, and 1975, as having been timely for their lack of fulfillment.

> Jesus tells us: "Keep looking, keep awake, for you do not know when the appointed time is. . . . Keep on the watch." (Mark 13:32-37) What if, in expectation of the "great tribulation," Jehovah's Witnesses had eased up, and stopped watching and making plans for the future, in 1914, in 1925, in 1975 or at any other date—could this have resulted in the expansive spiritual paradise that we see today? How glad we are that Jehovah has energized his people to keep sounding forth good news in all the earth![15]

Does the Watch Tower organization's version of the good news of God's kingdom resemble the good news as taught by Jesus and His disciples? Does it match what Christian have understood and taught about the gospel throughout the centuries? Jesus said in Matthew 24:26,27 to beware of those announcing a secret presence: "Wherefore if they shall say unto you, 'Behold, he is in the desert,' go not forth; 'Behold, he is in the secret chambers,' believe it not. For as the lightning cometh out of the east and shineth even unto the west, so shall also the coming of the Son of man be"(KJV).

The Watch Tower organization's good news is that Christ came invisibly and secretly in 1914, and only the Witnesses recognized this. Jesus said in Matthew 24:36,44 that no one would know the day or the hour of His coming. If they would not know the day or hour, how could someone specify the year that He came invisibly? "But of that day and hour no one knows, not even the angels of heaven, nor the Son, but the Father alone. For this reason you be ready too; for the Son of Man is coming at an hour when you do not think He will."

The Scriptures clearly teach that Christ's death is an atonement for sin. This is certainly good news. The Witnesses contend that the death of Christ merely opens the way for them to work out their salvation.

Jesus never taught that God's kingdom was a government composed of Himself and 144,000 co-rulers from the earth. He never taught a two-stage coming with a protracted invisible presence culminating in a destructive cataclysim. He never taught that His heavenly bride of associates would engage in a cleansing and perfecting of mankind. He did not teach that there would be two classes of believers—heavenly and earthly. He certainly never taught that God's kingdom rule would not have His personal visible oversight here on the planet but instead would be ruled by Witness elders or "princes" during the millennial reign. And He most certainly did not suggest that people would be separated into two classes of sheep and goats based on a parabolic faithful and discreet slave's spiritual food as offered and served by door-to-door consumer/publishers.

Indeed, the good news or gospel of the kingdom that Jehovah's Witnesses offer is very different from that offered by Jesus Christ and His disciples. It is unscriptural and therefore accursed, according to Galatians 1:8. Let the reader be warned of this false gospel.

10

Savior Angel

In the previous chapter we demonstrated that the gospel of Jehovah's Witnesses is a counterfeit compared to that of biblical Christianity. This leads us to naturally ask another question: What does the Watch Tower Society teach about Jesus?

A person who is initially exploring the Witnesses will not immediately learn what is really believed about Jesus. The use of familiar Christian terminology might lead some to believe that the Witnesses' Jesus is the same as the traditional Jesus. But that is not the case. The Jesus of the Watch Tower is actually Michael the archangel!

The Society teaches that Michael was the first born or first created of God. As a co-worker with God, he created all other things in the universe, including other angels as well as the planets and everything on them, including man. In order to ransom mankind from the sin of Adam, Michael willingly gave up spirit life when God transferred his life force to Mary's womb. He was born a perfect human, the man Jesus—nothing more than a man, nothing less than a man. He was the perfect counterpart of Adam, the first man. Jesus lived his life, fulfilled his ministry, and died faithful to God in his assigned role, without sinning. His body was not resurrected but was disposed of by God while in the tomb. God then re-created him as a spirit creature, who then materialized a number of times before the disciples. Finally he dematerialized as he ascended back to heaven, where once again he became Michael the archangel.

We are aware that this all seems very unusual to the average

145

reader. However, unorthodox ideas about Jesus are the norm among pseudo-Christian groups. While being filmed for the documentary *Witnesses of Jehovah*, two Watch Tower officials had this to say:

F.M. Gipe said:

> Our teaching on Jesus Christ is that Jesus is the son of God. He was the first thing that Jehovah created and through him other creative works were done. Now some religions teach that God and Jesus are one and the same, but the Bible does not teach that, and therefore neither do Jehovah's Witnesses.

Eugene Mortenson added:

> We believe that the Bible teaches that Jesus carries out a number of functions for Jehovah God the Most High. For an example, in the Hebrew scriptures he is referred to as Michael. Michael, literally translated into English, means "who is like God." He being the chief vindicator of Jehovah God's name. Also the Bible refers to him as the Word of God, and in the Bible, these names identify their function or their activities that they engage in. Being the "Word" of God means he is the spokesman for God.

A Watch Tower publication expands on what they said:

> The features as noted about this "strong angel" combine to indicate that he represents or stands for the glorified Lord Jesus Christ, who before his human birth was the archangel Michael. . . . Is there any question as to who is this Michael the archangel? He is no one else but Jesus Christ the only-begotten Son of God! He is the one who, before our Common Era began, was the heavenly prince of Jehovah's people,

including Daniel. Never did he renounce the right to that heavenly name, even when he became a perfect man here on earth in order to work for the interests of God's Messianic kingdom and to ransom all mankind by offering himself to God for a perfect human sacrifice. After his resurrection from the dead and his return to heaven, he resumed that heavenly name.[1]

The Watch Tower teaches that before being born on earth as a man, Jesus existed in heaven as a mighty spirit creature created by God.[2] He was known as the Word of God as well as God's "firstborn" and His "only-begotten" son. To Witnesses, this means that he was created before all the other spirit sons of God, and he is the only being directly created by God.[3]

So the organization believes that the Word who became Jesus was created at some distant time in the past. But where does the "Michael the archangel" connection come in? At this point it is necessary to go to the Scriptures to see if there is some verse that says or might imply that Jesus is Michael. The Bible notes a number of individuals who were named Michael—for example, Jehoshaphat's son, prince of Judah. However, the personage known as Michael the archangel is mentioned only five times in the Bible.

The first reference is Daniel 10:13, where he is referred to as "one of the chief princes." Later, in verse 21 of Daniel 10, he is called "Michael your prince." In Daniel 12:1 we read of "Michael, the great prince who stands guard over the sons of your people." The two other references are in the New Testament. In Jude 9 we read about "Michael the archangel, when he disputed with the devil" and in Revelation 12:7 we read about "Michael and his angels waging war with the dragon."

Not one of these verses say that Michael the archangel is Jesus! Although this is merely a theory they totally endorse the idea as fact. If an individual Jehovah's Witness would disagree and be vocal about it, he would be subject to disfellowshipment.

In their publication *Reasoning From The Scriptures* published in 1985, the Watch Tower organization addresses the question "Is

Jesus Christ the same person as Michael the archangel?" on page 218. Besides mentioning the five verses that we have cited, it notes 1 Thessalonians 4:16—"the command of Jesus Christ for the resurrection to begin is described as 'the archangel's call' "—and then makes the connection to Jude 9 to identify the archangel as Michael:

> Would it be appropriate to liken Jesus' commanding call to that of someone lesser in authority? Reasonably, then, the archangel Michael is Jesus Christ. (Interestingly, the expression "archangel" is never found in the plural in the Scriptures, thus implying that there is only one.)
>
> Revelation 12:7-12 says that Michael and his angels would war against Satan and hurl him and his wicked angels out of heaven in connection with the conferring of kingly authority on Christ. Jesus is later depicted as leading the armies of heaven in war against the nations of the world. (Rev. 19:11-16) Is it not reasonable that Jesus would also be the one to take action against the one he described as "ruler of this world," Satan the Devil? (John 12:31) Daniel 12:1 (RS) associates the "standing up of Michael" to act with authority with "a time of trouble, such as never has been since there was a nation till that time." That would certainly fit the experience of the nations when Christ as heavenly executioner takes action against them. So the evidence indicates that the Son of God was known as Michael before he came to earth and is known also by that name since his return to heaven where he resides as the glorified spirit Son of God.

Just where is the scriptural exegesis for the conclusions reached by the Watch Tower leadership? Their explanation is filled with terms like "evidently," "reasonably," "appropriate," "certainly," and "evidence," as if these terms should convince us when the evidence does not. Is not their explanation nothing more than supposition and rationalism run amok?

For example, they conclude that 1 Thessalonians 4:16 supports their Jesus/Michael theory. But does it? The text of 1 Thessalonians 4:16 reads, "For the Lord Himself will descend from heaven with a shout, with the voice of the archangel, and with the trumpet of God; and the dead in Christ shall rise first." The Scripture refers to the second coming of the Lord Jesus, "when every eye shall see him." Matthew 24:31 describes some of the events that will take place: "He will send forth His angels with a great trumpet and they will gather together His elect from the four winds, from one end of the sky to the other."

When 1 Thessalonians 4:16 states "with a shout" it does not refer to Jesus shouting. Rather, it means that He will be attended with a shout, as with a multitude or army rushing to a conflict. Interestingly, the Greek word used here is not used elsewhere in the New Testament. It denotes a cry of excitement, or of urging on; an outcry, clamor, as of soldiers rushing to battle.

The passage goes on to say "with the voice of the archangel," and this too does not say that it is Jesus' voice. Second Thessalonians 1:7 says in part, ". . . when the Lord Jesus shall be revealed from heaven with His mighty angels in flaming fire." If Jesus brings an army of mighty angels with Him on that glorious occasion, would it not be appropriate that His chief angel, the archangel Michael, accompany Him? The answer is yes, and Michael's voice is part of the loud shout or cry that will be made by the descending hosts of heaven. It could also be that Michael's voice is used for the purpose of summoning the world to judgment. However, his voice cannot be used to raise the dead, for that will be by the "voice of the Son of God" (John 5:25,28,29). Therefore it is not the "voice of the archangel" that commands the resurrection to begin.[4]

The latter part of 1 Thessalonians 4:16, "with the trumpet of God," refers to the trumpet which God appoints to be sounded. It does not say that God sounds it Himself.

Many Witnesses are embarrassed by the Jesus/Michael doctrine and go out of their way to avoid discussing it. The doctrine is impossible to explain without all kinds of Watch Tower commentary.

Orthodox Christianity teaches that the Word was God (John 1:1) and incarnated as Jesus Christ, who upon His resurrection ascended back into heaven. The Watch Tower teaches that the Word was Michael the archangel, who gave up heavenly existence when God transferred his life force to the egg cell in the womb of Mary. He ceased to exist as a spirit creature. He was not an incarnation of Michael:

> When God's "firstborn" came to earth, the life force of the Word was transferred from heaven to the egg cell in the womb of Mary. This meant that the Word had to lay aside his heavenly glory, his spirit life. . . . When the Word "became flesh" he was no longer a spirit creature.[5]
>
> He was no incarnation of a heavenly person, no incarnation of the "Word of God."[6]

Thus the Watch Tower teaches that this was not an incarnation. Michael went out of existence and the transferred life force became a perfect human man.

> Because he was a perfect man, even as Adam had been, Jesus is called "the last Adam." No human other than Jesus could have provided the ransom. This is because Jesus is the only man who ever lived that was equal to Adam as a perfect human son of God.[7]
>
> Yes, he was no incarnation or materialization of a spirit person to a fleshly body parading as a man during his 33 1/2-year residence on earth in the flesh. He was a perfect man, having a perfect human body of flesh and blood, a perfect human organism.[8]

In other words, the man Jesus was energized by the life force of Michael the archangel and Michael was erased, at least during the time Jesus was on earth.

Jehovah's Witnesses also teach a different resurrection. Orthodox Christianity teaches the bodily resurrection of Jesus. Witnesses teach that Jesus' body was disposed of by God—that it was dissolved or disintegrated.

> What happened to the perfect fleshly body of Jesus after his death? Was it preserved so that in time men will look upon it in worship? or does Jesus still have this fleshly body in the heavens, "spiritualized" so that it can be seen and worshiped? Neither. The Scriptures answer: It was disposed of by Jehovah God, dissolved into its constituent elements or atoms. . . . The Devil wanted to obtain the fleshly body of Jesus after his death to induce some to worship it and use it for indecent false religious purposes, thus reproaching Jehovah God. . . . So God caused Jesus' body to disappear, but not corrupt, meaning that it was dissolved, disintegrated back into the elements from which all human bodies are made.[9]

This blatantly contradicts the Scriptures. They testify not that Jesus' body would be disintegrated, but that it would be raised from the dead! Jesus Himself prophesied in John 2:19, "Destroy this temple, and in three days I will raise it up." Verse 21 confirms that He was speaking about His physical body being raised from the dead.

Jehovah's Witnesses are taught that instead of a resurrection, God re-created Jesus. Charles Russell taught this a hundred years ago[10] and the concept continues to this very day:

> Do you know what happened to Jesus' body? God caused it to disappear. God did not raise Jesus to life in

the fleshly body in which he died. He gave Jesus a new
spirit body, as the angels in heaven have.[11]

The teaching goes that Jesus now had a new spirit body. He
materialized at various times and occasions to his disciples, and
his physical appearance varied, for at times his followers did not
recognize him.[12]

Finally, after Jesus' ascension to heaven, he once again became
Michael the archangel, while retaining the name Jesus. After
leaving the sight of his followers, he dematerialized, never to be
seen again:

> He resumed his heavenly name Michael. The name
> Jesus Christ was retained in order to show his identi-
> calness with the human-born Son of God on earth.
> The name Michael was resumed in order to tie him in
> with his prehuman existence.[13]

To recap, the Watch Tower organization teaches that Jesus was
not an incarnation of God the Son but rather that he has existed in
the form of three separate entities. Entity one, a created Word/
Michael, goes out of existence, when his life force is transferred
to entity two, the man Jesus, who upon his death is disintegrated
and re-created as entity three, a new spirit being who then
re-enters heaven to become Michael the archangel again. The
Watchtower emphatically states that "never at any time has Jesus
been equal to his Father but is ever subordinate to him."[14]

Watch Tower leadership claims that the incarnation of Jesus is
confusing and contradictory:

> Incarnation is the teaching in Christendom that
> "God is Man and Man is God in the Person of Jesus
> Christ." This belief is called "the central doctrine of
> Christianity." Catholic and most Protestant churches
> thus teach that Jesus was a God-Man. But, like other
> doctrines taught by the clergy, this one, too, defies

logic and reason. Indeed, theologians admit that no human philosophy can fully explain it. It is contradictory and it is confusing.[15]

We must admit that the doctrine of Jesus as God/man is difficult for our human minds to fully grasp. But contradictory and confusing? Is not the Watch Tower theory of "Word/Michael-Jesus-Jesus/Michael" the one that is contradictory and confusing?

Grandfather God

If the Michael/Jesus doctrine isn't enough, consider the teaching that we have two heavenly fathers. In Isaiah 9:6 we read, "For a child will be born to us, a son will be given to us; and the government will rest on His shoulders; and His name will be called Wonderful Counselor, Mighty God, Eternal Father, Prince of Peace." This Scripture applies to Jesus Christ and assures us that He is our Mighty God and Eternal Father.

The Watch Tower published a new book in 1986 entitled *Worldwide Security Under The "Prince of Peace"* This publication introduced a new "member" to the Jehovah's Witness family. The book outlines the concept that Jehovah's Witnesses have TWO GODS—Jesus as the "Mighty God" and Jehovah as the "Almighty God." We have already seen that Jehovah's Witnesses have TWO MOTHERS—their "earthly" mother organization and their "heavenly" mother organization. According to this publication they also have TWO FATHERS. On page 163 they explain:

The Son of God is to become the "Eternal Father" to this human family, for which he laid down his perfect human life in sacrifice.

This presents a problem, because mankind also has the eternal Father that Jesus taught his followers to pray to. This is handled by calling Jesus an *adoptive* Father (page 164). The Witnesses then establish a new relationship between God the Father and restored mankind. He now becomes their *Grandfather*! Page 169 of the same book states:

> . . . the heavenly Father of Jesus Christ will become the heavenly Grandfather of the restored human family. For this reason the human family will enter into a new relationship with the Creator of heaven and earth.

Isaiah 9:6 states that Jesus is mankind's Eternal Father. However, using Watch Tower logic, Jesus is not the *Eternal* Father at all, because at the end of the thousand-year millennium he hands everything over to his heavenly Father Jehovah. Page 181 of *Worldwide Security Under the "Prince of Peace"*:

> When the "Prince of Peace" hands over the Kingdom of his God at the end of the Thousand Year Reign, earth's inhabitants will be made aware of this act of their adoptive Father. With him as their Royal Example, they will likewise subject themselves in a new aspect to the Most High God. Now for the first time they will render loving submission directly to Jehovah, yes, worship, in all sincerity and truth, no longer requiring the priestly services of Jesus, not even when praying.

So when Jesus hands the kingdom over to his Father, he relinquishes his role as mankind's adoptive Father. Jehovah now gives up His position of Grandfather and resumes His position as restored mankind's heavenly Father. This conglomeration of Gods, Mothers, Fathers, and Grandfather resembles Greek mythology more than biblical Christianity.

Two Classes

In the previous chapter we described the Witness teaching about the 144,000 bride-of-Christ class. The teaching about

Jesus combined with the 144,000 creates a unique "two-class" religion. Only the elect class of 144,000 are born again and go to heaven. They are referred to at various times as "the anointed," "the remnant," "the spiritual temple class," "spiritual Israelites," "spiritual priests," "Jesus' spiritual brothers," "spirit-begotten sons of God," "the promised seed of the woman," "associate king-priests," "chosen ones," "heavenly joint heirs," "immortal joint heirs," and "underpriests." Some of these titles apply once they have died and gone to heaven to rule with Christ. According to the Watch Tower Society's statistics, there are approximately 9000 of this chosen class alive today.

The secondary class of believers are known simply as the "great crowd" or "other sheep." According to Watch Tower statistics, they number about 3.4 million at this writing. They have no heavenly hope but will remain on earth forever if they are faithful to Jehovah and His organization.

There is an additional group of persons associated with the Watch Tower organization who are not counted as Jehovah's Witnesses in the classic sense of being a consumer/publisher. These people, numbering approximately 5 million, are studying to become a Witness or in some other way have a relationship with the Witnesses. But unless they are baptized and become active in door-to-door witnessing, they have no eternal hope.

Once a year Jehovah's Witnesses and their invited friends and associates gather to commemorate the Lord's evening meal—commonly called communion among Christians. Of the approximately 8 million persons worldwide who gather that evening, only the 9000 members of the "anointed remnant" partake of the unleavened bread and wine when it is passed! All other persons in attendance are merely observers. The vast majority of congregations do not have a single person partake because there are 52,000 congregations.

Simple arithmetic shows the incongruity of the matter. In fact the whole "memorial celebration" is nothing more than a parody of what Jesus instituted at His last supper with the apostles. The Scriptures state plainly that those persons in the new covenant should indeed partake of the Lord's evening meal. First Corinthians 11:24,25 quotes these words of Jesus: "This is My body, which is for you; do this in remembrance of Me," and "This cup is the new covenant in My blood; do this, as often as you drink it, in remembrance of Me." The invitation to all born-again Christians is to partake of communion, or the Lord's evening meal. This is to continue until the Lord returns (1 Corinthians 11:26).

The question then becomes, Why do these select Jehovah's Witnesses partake of the Lord's evening meal when they believe He has already come invisibly in 1914? Also, where in the written Word of God does it say that those not in the new covenant are supposed to gather once a year and observe a few individuals consume a piece of unleavened bread and drink a little wine? Indeed, most Jehovah's Witnesses gather merely to pass the bread and wine, with no one partaking! Should a Witness not be present at the memorial celebration on Nisan 14, he is considered "spiritually weak." Should an elder or ministerial servant not attend, his position of oversight would be in jeopardy. The only exception is if the Witness is confined to bed because of illness or injury, or if he is away from his home congregation, in which case he is expected to locate a Kingdom Hall of Jehovah's Witnesses and participate there.

This lifeless ceremony is the only "celebration" that a Witness is required to attend. All other celebrations or holidays held dear by most Christians are forbidden, and a Jehovah's Witness can be disfellowshipped for celebrating them. (The only other celebration not forbidden is the marriage anniversary. Witness couples are given the choice of celebrating or not, based upon their conscience on the matter.)

To add further condemnation to the Watch Tower leadership that dreams up these heresies, they have restricted the new covenant to 144,000 persons. Thus they deprive millions of their followers from a personal relationship with Jesus Christ. They teach two hopes and two classes. The Bible teaches one hope and one calling. Ephesians 4:4-6 says, "There is one body and one Spirit, just as also you were called in one hope of your calling;

one Lord, one faith, one baptism, one God and Father of all who is over all and through all and in all."

Jehovah's Witnesses are also taught that Christ's role in the plan of salvation does not fully cover all of mankind. In *The Watchtower* article quoted below, notice that they have added in parenthesis "not, *all* men," thereby directly contradicting the Word of God.

> What, then, is Christ's role in this program of salvation? Paul proceeds to say: "There is one God, and one mediator between God and men [not, *all* men], a man Christ Jesus, who gave himself a corresponding ransom for all." 1 Tim. 2:5,6[16]

The "anointed class" are the only ones for whom Jesus is a direct mediator. The "other sheep" benefit only in a relative way. They have a "relatively righteous standing before him."[17] The vast majority of Jehovah's Witnesses, professing to be Christian, gather once a year to refuse the bread and wine of communion. This is nothing more than a bizarre parody of what Christ instituted.

> Those who are not in the new covenant and who have not been taken by Jesus into a covenant for a kingdom do not partake of the Memorial emblems, but they still should recognize how important to them Jesus' sacrificed flesh and blood are. This sacrifice is the means whereby they can gain everlasting life on earth.[18]

The "other sheep" enjoy a relative relationship with Jesus and must continue to work out their salvation both before and after Armageddon. Jesus' sacrifice has only a relative merit, in that the Watch Tower organization teaches that Jesus' sacrifice only canceled Adamic sin. The "other sheep" are still responsible for their own sins and must earn merit with God by continuing faithful until a final test of their integrity at the end of the thousand-year millennial reign.

We have shown that the Watch Tower teaches a different gospel, a different Jesus, and a different salvation from the Bible and orthodox Christianity. It is not our purpose to belittle or insult the Witnesses; however, their leadership has erroneously taught them that their savior is a superangel who has provided only a partial, relative atonement. Their leadership has also persuaded them to believe that eternal life through Jesus Christ, as presented in the Holy Bible, is not for them.

Jesus therefore said to them, "Truly, truly, I say to you, unless you eat the flesh of the Son of Man and drink His blood, you have no life in yourselves. He who eats My flesh and drinks My blood has eternal life, and I will raise him up on the last day. For My flesh is true food, and My blood is true drink. He who eats My flesh and drinks My blood abides in Me, and I in him. As the living Father sent Me, and I live because of the Father, so he who eats Me, he also shall live because of Me. This is the bread which came down out of heaven; not as the fathers ate, and died, he who eats this bread shall live forever" (John 6:53-58).

11

The Occult Connection

While I was an elder of a Kingdom Hall in San Diego, I received a call from a woman who was studying with some Witnesses in my congregation. Over the years she had obtained a significant collection of Chinese antiques, including some valuable Foo Dogs. The Witness women were encouraging her to destroy these pagan objects because they could attract demons, and she wanted to know what I thought she should do.

"Have you had any strange occurrences in your house?" I asked. "Any rappings or voices or unusual things like that?"

"No, not at all," she answered.

I explained to her that there had been cases of objects being used by demons to influence people. When that happened, we encouraged them to destroy the objects in order to break the spell. However, since nothing unusual had happened in her home, she certainly should not listen to the advice of these women.

At first this situation may sound somewhat bizarre. How could anyone suggest that this lady destroy such a valuable art collection? But to Jehovah's Witnesses, there is a strange preoccupation with anything remotely related to demons. Persons who oppose the Watch Tower are referred to as "demonized." Should a Witness develop a nervous condition, the demons are immediately suspect. Demons continually come up in normal conversation among the Witnesses. Their literature and discourses also make reference to demons on a continual basis. In the Watch Tower Publications Index, published in 1986, there are approximately 5000 references to the occult.

Psychologist Jerry Bergman, for many years a Jehovah's Witness, has written a book titled *The Mental Health of Jehovah's Witnesses*. While interviewing him for the film *Witnesses of Jehovah*, he told us this tragic story. It was about a Witness who was very active in his congregation for many years. When he started to behave very strangely, the elders thought that the furniture in his house was demonized, since he had bought it from the Salvation Army. So they began to burn pieces of his furniture in order to destroy this demon influence. Eventually they burned nearly every piece of furniture in his house, but the man showed no improvement. In fact he was getting worse.

The elders then started to burn the man's clothing and other possessions, including family portraits. Through Dr. Bergman's encouragement, the elders finally took the man to a medical doctor. The doctor ordered tests at a hospital, where it was diagnosed that the patient had a brain tumor and would require immediate surgery. However, the man died before the operation could be performed.

To understand the Witnesses' obsession with demons, we need to go back to the very first issue of *Zion's Watch Tower*, authored by Charles Taze Russell. Under the heading "What is Truth," Russell stated, "A *truth* presented by Satan himself is just *as true* as a *truth* stated by God." He went on to chastise Christians for ignoring truth presented by their opponents and urged readers to "accept truth wherever you find it."

The problem with this statement is that it contradicts the spoken words of Jesus Christ. In John 8:44 He warns us about Satan's truth: "He was a murderer from the beginning, and does not stand in the truth, because there is no truth in him. Whenever he speaks a lie, he speaks from his own nature; for he is a liar, and the father of lies."

It was this kind of faulty reasoning—that unbelievers and even Satan himself can be looked to for truths that are then "reconciled" and "harmonized" with biblical truth—that caused young Russell to open himself to all kinds of heretical teachings. That remains the case today, as we will see shortly.

Early Manifestations

The preoccupation with spiritism and occultic demonism goes back to Russell. He spoke and wrote so extensively against involvement in spiritism or occult practices that his followers became thoroughly paranoid. He taught that demons were materializing and causing all sorts of havoc, thus opening an era of intense spiritistic activity among his followers.

As the critical year of 1914 approached, the Bible Students reported all manner of manifestations of spirits. Russell wrote concerning this in *Zion's Watch Tower* of October 1, 1907:

> Our understanding is that this great day of the Lord began chronologically in October, 1874, and from what we can learn it is since that date that "materializations" have become more and more common . . . the evidence is too strong to be disputed that there have been numerous genuine manifestations—materializations—in which the spirit personating the dead has assumed a material body, possessing weight and various qualities similiar to a human. . . . A sister in the Truth who was at one time a spirit medium assures us that not long since in the parlor of her own home, the door being shut, a spirit materialized before her in the form of a man who spoke to her. His request being refused, he threateningly caught her by the arm with a firm grasp, but at that instant her brother opened the parlor door and the materialization instantly dissolved.[1]

Russell cited two other dramatic examples, then went on to sternly warn the Bible Students to have nothing to do with spirit mediums, seances, hypnotism, or other forms of spiritism. Later he pressured his members to take a vow that included the following statement: "I vow to thee that I will be on the alert to resist everything akin to Spiritism and Occultism, and that remembering that there are but the two masters, I shall resist these snares in all reasonable ways, as being of the adversary." In time this vow gained the status of a talisman to ward off evil spirits.

Despite his staunch opposition to anything hinting of the demonic, he printed a letter in the May 1, 1912, *Watch Tower* in which the writer explained that an evil spirit he had contacted had confirmed that Pastor Russell's *Millennial Dawn* series of books (later renamed *Studies in the Scriptures*) were correct in doctrine as well as in chronology. Apparently this would include all of his Pyramid teaching. In other words, the demons endorsed Russell's theology!

Cover-Up

Today, as in Russell's time, the Watch Tower Society goes to great lengths to denounce spiritistic practices. However, do they really believe that all contacts with spirits is wrong? Or do they in fact utilize the teachings of the spirit world to endorse their beliefs?

In 2 Corinthians 11:13-15 the apostle Paul warns that false prophets are disguising themselves as apostles of Christ: "And no wonder, for even Satan disguises himself as an angel of light. Therefore it is not suprising if his servants also disguise themselves as servants of righteousness." The Watch Tower organization likes to present itself as a champion of truth and an enemy of darkness. Yet it has used the teachings of spirit mediums to support its doctrines. This is in direct conflict with commands in Scripture such as Leviticus 19:31—"Do not turn to mediums or spiritists; do not seek them out to be defiled by them. I am the Lord your God."

Of course, the organization uses very clever tactics, as we shall see. In the April 1, 1983, issue of *The Watchtower*, an interesting question was raised in the section "Questions from Readers": "Why, in recent years, has *The Watchtower* not made use of the translation by the former Catholic priest, Johannes Greber?" The following answer was given on page 31:

This translation was used occasionally in support of renderings of Matthew 27:52,53 and John 1:1. . . . But as indicated in a foreword to the 1980 edition of *The New Testament* by Johannes Greber, this translator relied on "God's Spirit World" to clarify for him how he should translate difficult passages. It is stated: "His wife, a medium of God's Spiritworld, was often instrumental in conveying the correct answers from God's messengers to Pastor Greber." *The Watchtower* has deemed it improper to make use of a translation that has such a close rapport with spiritism.

The question might be asked, What precipitated this explanation? Was this merely an ongoing corrective measure designed to purify the publications of the Watch Tower? In fact, it was nothing more than a smokescreen designed to cover up the fact that they had used The New Testament translated by Johannes Greber as an authority for years!

The explanation was needed because of pressure from outside sources who had discovered the flagrant use of a spirit medium's translation of the Bible and were exposing this in print. To counteract this exposure, the leadership presented the impression that they had only recently discovered this little error and corrected it. In fact, pressure had been building on this issue for some time, and they could no longer ignore it.

Just who was Johannes Greber, and why should we be concerned about him? The promotional material produced by the Johannes Greber Memorial Foundation tells us that he was born in Germany in 1874 and was ordained a Catholic priest in 1900. About that time he started to attend seances and communicate with "spirits." Quoting from a brochure promoting his book *Communication with the Spirit World of God*, we find the following:

> Late in the summer of 1923 God's holy spirits contacted Pastor Greber. They revealed great truths to him and approximately two-and-one-half years later he was given permanent leave from the church. . . .

The brochure goes on to tell how Greber translated the New Testament. It says that through constant prayer for guidance, "God's Spirit World" clarified discrepancies and contradictions between the ancient scrolls and modern versions of the New Testament.

> At times he was given the correct answers in large illuminated letters and words passing before his eyes. Other times he was given the correct answers during prayer meetings. His wife, a medium of God's Spirit World, was often instrumental in conveying the correct answers from God's Messengers to Pastor Greber.

It is very clear that the source of Greber's enlightenment was not God. Nevertheless, the Watch Tower organization quoted Greber's translation as an authority for its doctrines. They would have us believe that they only recently became aware of Greber's spiritistic connections. In fact, they knew about them as early as 1956! In an article entitled "Triumphing Over Wicked Spirit Forces" in the February 15, 1956, *Watchtower*, they discuss Johannes Greber, quoting him concerning his communication with the spirit world on pages 110 and 111. Commenting on Greber's New Testament, they wrote: "Very plainly the spirits in which ex-priest Greber believes helped him in his translation."

In spite of that realization, they proceeded to quote him as an authority on biblical interpretation on at least seven occasions between 1962 and 1982.[2]

The reason why the Watch Tower Society would resort to using a translation by an avowed spirit medium is because they cannot find recognized and legitimate Bible translators to lend authority to their doctrines. Interestingly, the translation of Johannes Greber corresponds very closely to the Watch Tower's own *New World Translation*.

The Watch Tower organization concedes that spiritism should not be a source for knowledge, yet it uses that very source to substantiate its theology. In the October 15, 1977, *Watchtower*, on page 624, the following self-incriminating statement was made:

> Since spiritism is condemned by God, it becomes obvious that a person appealing to spiritism for knowledge or help is not appealing to God. He is looking to a source opposed to God. . . .

It is an incredible contradiction to condemn anything having to do with spiritism while at the same time quoting from mediumistic sources to support doctrine. Lest this might be excused as a small slipup or error on the part of Watch Tower writers, it must be remembered that Greber's translation was used at least seven times. In an attempt to minimize this matter, the Watch Tower's "Ministry of Truth" did some editing work.

In 1986 the organization published a new *Publications Index* covering the years 1930 through 1985. They claim that this Index "embodies all previously published Indexes." Subjects are listed under main headings and information is classified by subject. On page 372, under the heading GREBER, JOHANNES, we find the reference to the "Questions from Readers" article of April 1, 1983, page 31, and one reference to John 1:1 in the 1962 *Watchtower* on page 554. The other six times Greber was used are simply deleted!

There is very good reason for this, of course. Should a Witness be confronted by a knowledgeable person concerning the Watch Tower's use of a spirit medium, and should that Witness decide to do some research, he would find only the two notations in his Index. Naturally, he would conclude that Watch Tower writers used Greber as a source only once, then discovered their mistake. It all appears rather innocuous.

Shocking Parallels

It is also revealing to note that a number of Watch Tower doctrines line up with what Greber's spirit messengers revealed to him as "truth" in his book *Communication with the Spirit World of God*. Frequently throughout his book Greber quotes verbatim from his spirit messengers. The following are a few quotes from *Communications with the Spirit World of God* followed by equivalent teachings of the Watch Tower:

Communication with the Spirit World of God, page 333:

> Christ's contention concerning His own person, concerning the source of His doctrine and the power which He possessed was, therefore, that He had received each and everything from the Father. From Himself He had nothing. *He is not God.*

Reasoning from the Scriptures, page 214:

> And Jesus himself never claimed to be God but, rather, "the *Son* of God." Jesus was sent into the world by God; so by means of this only-begotten Son, God was with mankind.

Communication with the Spirit World of God, page 371:

> As you see, the doctrine of a triune Godhead is not only contrary to common sense, but is entirely unsupported by the Scriptures.

Reasoning from the Scriptures, page 424:

> The evidence is indisputable that the dogma of the Trinity is not found in the Bible, nor is it in harmony with what the Bible teaches.

Communication with the Spirit World of God, page 364:

> That Christ is not God I proved to you by the Scriptures and in greater detail, when I taught you concerning His life and His work.

The truth that only the Father, but not the Son, is God, is furthermore sustained by the teachings of the Apostles. Thus Paul writes: ". . . there is no God, but one."

The Watchtower, December 1, 1983, page 16:

Consistently Paul makes this distinction not only between the Father and Jesus but between *God* and Jesus. He writes of God *and* Christ.

Communication with the Spirit World of God, pages 385-86:

To the Christians of today the "resurrection of the dead" means the making anew of the physical body, and Christ's resurrection on Easter Sunday is regarded by them as the reunion of His spirit with His body which had lain in its grave for three days. . . . *Not even of Christ was the natural body raised.* Like the physical bodies of all mortals it had been created from the od of the earth and like them it returned to earth, with this exception, that it was not redissolved into terrestrial od by way of decay, but by dematerialization effected by the spirit-world.

Aid to Bible Understanding, pages 247, 587, 1587:

When his disciples went to the tomb early on the first day of the week, Jesus' body had disappeared and the grave clothes were left in the tomb, his body doubtless being disintegrated without passing through the process of decaying. . . . Jehovah God evidently disposed of Jesus' fleshly body in his own way (possibly disintegrating it into the atoms of which it was constituted). . . . he was resurrected, but not in his fleshly body, which was given as a ransom sacrifice;

yet that fleshly body did not go into corruption, but was disposed of by God. . . .

Communication with the Spirit World of God, page 285:

Erring mortals revised the Biblical accounts, omitting what they could not understand or adding their own mistaken explanations. . . . Elsewhere in the Holy Writ the truth has suffered at the hands of translators who have rendered certain words and phrases of the original text so inadequately as to distort their real meaning beyond recognition.

The New Testament, by Johannes Greber, page 8:

It is an actual fact that no other book on earth has undergone so many changes and falsifications at the hands of the copyists as has the Bible. . . . Even the well versed scholar cannot say for certain. . . which of the words, sentences, or chapters that have been intentionally or accidentally left out, overlooked, misread, misinterpreted, capriciously altered, or deliberately falsified by the copyists . . . the situation is made worse by the translations of the text into our modern languages.

All Scripture Is Inspired Of God And Beneficial, page 323:

. . . all these translations, even down to the very latest, have their defects. There are inconsistencies or unsatisfactory renderings, infected with sectarian traditions or worldly philosophies, and hence not in full harmony with the sacred truths that Jehovah has recorded in his Word.

We could give many more examples. The similarities between what the spirit messengers taught Johannes Greber and what the

Watch Tower Society teaches are remarkable. No wonder we are warned not to have any contact with spiritism, for the truth cannot be found there!

Here We Go Again

With the admission that Greber's work was directed by "spirits," the Watch Tower had to find another authority for some of their unorthodox teachings. A classic example concerns their rendering of John 1:1. The New American Standard Bible renders the verse "In the beginning was the Word, and the Word was with God, and the Word was God." This verse is one of the strong statements in the Bible concerning the deity of Jesus Christ, and all legitimate, recognized translations have a similar rendering. However, the Watch Tower renders the last phrase "and the Word was a god." In other words, he is a lesser god— one of many. This effectively denigrates Christ's deity. Greber's New Testament translation of John 1:1 supported the "a god" teaching.

In the 1985 edition of *The Kingdom Interlinear Translation of the Greek Scriptures*, the Watch Tower has provided an elaborate appendix at the back. On pages 1139 and 1140 they tender new support for their "a god" translation of John 1:1. They use as an authority John S. Thompson of Baltimore, who wrote *The Monotessaron*, or *The Gospel History, According to the Four Evangelists*, in 1829.

The American Quarterly Review of September 1830, volume 8, pages 227 through 245, provides us with some interesting facts concerning John S. Thompson. He apparently was not a modest man, for in his autobiographic statement in the *Review* he states, "I shall rejoice in having been the happy instrument, in the hand of God, of having done fourfold as much for mankind, as all the professed commentators of the last fifteen centuries!"

A religious eclectic, Thompson changed from Calvinism to Arminianism, becoming a Methodist preacher. Then the *Review* goes on to state that he became a Restorationist, then an Arian

Restorationist, and finally, by the time he wrote his volume in 1829, he had become a Unitarian Universalist! Thompson, like Greber and Greber's "spirit messengers," held the clergy in low regard: "The meanest being on earth stands higher, in my approbation, than a deceitful, whining preacher! And I verily believe, I and God are of one opinion on this subject."

Perhaps the most interesting similarity between Thompson and Greber is the source of their inspiration and direction—the spirit world. Thompson describes a visit by one of these spirits: ". . . on retiring to rest, I enjoyed a return of the same happy and celestial influence. Whether in a dream or vision I was unable to determine; but I thought a seraph entered my room, filling it with a luminous effulgence, exceeding tenfold that of the sun: whilst I distinctly perceived . . . the apparition, I heard a voice, saying read 1 Kings III. 10, 11., and the room became gradually dark, as the light withdrew at one of the windows."

The spirits had instructions for Thompson, which he reveals in his account: "I awoke, one night, and heard a considerable noise in my room. I listened carefully for some time, and the sound was that of a thousand pens, writing in great haste what was dictated. I heard a voice very distinctly, saying,—'In all your writings, *be careful to represent Jesus as only the instrument of God in all he does.*' I immediately interrupted, by exclaiming,—'Silence! I'll not believe one of you.' The noise immediately stopped; and I was often afterward sorry that I had interrupted the dictation."

Though initially disturbed by the spirits' messages, Thompson finally comes under their power, for the above account continues, "Not long after, sleeping in the same room, I awoke by pressure, which removed immediately on awaking. I began to reflect, whether it was a dream, or an external force applied to my body. Whilst I doubted, some being took hold of my hands, and pressed them with violence, which excited in me great surprise. My hands were let loose, but, in one minute, they were again seized, with renewed violence. I then cried,—'Let me loose! I believe! do not injure me! I am entirely satisfied of your existence!' "

Apparently John S. Thompson took the advice of the "voice" which commanded him to "represent Jesus as only the instrument of God in all he does," for in the Watch Tower Society's *Kingdom Interlinear Translation*, 1985, on page 1139, Thompson's rendering of John 1:1 "and the Logos was a god" is quoted as an authority for their own "a god" teaching.

So in spite of the fact that the Watch Tower organization was caught red-handed in their use of a spirit medium's translation, and had to attempt a cover-up of the matter, we now find them once again using the translation of another "spirit"-directed authority.

The words of the apostle Paul in his first letter to Timothy are appropriate in closing:

> But the Spirit explicitly says that in later times some will fall away from the faith, paying attention to deceitful spirits and doctrines of demons (1 Timothy 4:1).

12

Life-and-Death Choices

In 1943 Leroy Gholson was working at his job at Marshall-Fields department store in Chicago when FBI agents arrived and took him away. This event was to have devastating, long-term effects on the Gholson family. Leroy had refused military service on the grounds that it would break his neutrality as one of Jehovah's Witnesses. For his stand he was sentenced to serve three years in the federal prison at Springfield, Missouri. Leroy was one of thousands of Jehovah's Witnesses who chose prison rather than join the military during World War II.

Fred Gholson, the second child of Leroy and his wife, Diane, was born a few months after his father was imprisoned. Fred told us in an interview that his childhood was basically nonexistent. All available time was occupied with meetings, door-to-door literature-selling, and preparations for either meetings or studies.

By the time Fred was 22, in 1966, the Vietnam War was raging and again the military issue confronted the Gholson family. As a sincere, dedicated Jehovah's Witness, Fred also refused to report for induction into the U.S. Armed Forces. As a result, he was indicted by a federal grand jury. Gholson was offered alternative service in a hospital, a civilian assignment in lieu of military service. However, this was also unacceptable because he still would have been under the jurisdiction of the military. Fred told us that his elders ruled that if the judge ordered him to go to work in the hospital, that would be all right according to the Witness rules—he would be under the authority of the courts and not the military. Unfortunately, he told this to the judge, and when he revealed this to the Witness overseers they said it would not be acceptable because this would be a compromise because the judge would not be acting upon his own volition!

The final irony was that Fred Gholson, like his father, was sentenced to three years in federal prison at Springfield, Missouri—the same prison in which his father, Leroy, had served his sentence over two decades earlier! There his job was to work as an orderly in the prison hospital in the contagious-disease section. His work as an orderly was exactly the same civilian job he had refused as alternative service.

Like thousands of Jehovah's Witnesses, Leroy and Fred Gholson carry the stigma of being a felon. For the rest of their lives this will be a blot on their records and hinder their job opportunities. But at least now they are no longer under the oppressive rule of the Watchtower. In the early 1980's Fred and his wife, Kate, as well as Fred's parents, Leroy and Diane, left the Watchtower movement.

This is just one example of the way Jehovah's Witnesses control the lives of their members. Critical decisions, at times literally life-and-death choices, are made for them without consideration for their wishes, conscience, or circumstances. If members disagree with these decisions, they are caught in a dilemma: If they act according to their conscience and defy Watchtower policy, they will be disfellowshipped and lose all contact with friends and loved ones.

Such rigidity is not always displayed on the part of policymakers. In fact, total reversals are not uncommon, and what once was a disfellowshipping offense becomes a matter of individual conscience, or vice versa. Sometimes the contradiction exists simultaneously. Such is the tragic case involving Witnesses in the countries of Malawi and Mexico.

In 1964 Jehovah's Witnesses in Malawi began to experience violent persecution. The persecution occurred again in 1967, 1972, and 1975. The issue centered around the purchase of a party identification card of the ruling political party. This was considered to be a breach of neutrality by the Watch Tower Society's Branch Office, even though there is only one ruling party in the country. The card was to be purchased by each citizen of the country for approximately 25 cents with the funds going for development projects of the country. The card itself holds about the same importance as a United States Social Security card, with no political overtones.

The Africans were intimidated into believing that those in possession of the cards would face destruction at Armageddon in 1975. The Witnesses refused to purchase the card and became in effect an opposition party of the lawful government. Word got out quickly, and bands of toughs and hoodlums took advantage of the situation. Atrocities followed. Witnesses had their homes sacked and burned, and their livestock looted. Some Witnesses were beaten to death. Thousands of women were stripped, beaten, and raped.

Witnesses fled Malawi into neighboring Mozambique, where they lived in refugee camps. Unfortunately, many received similar treatment to that encountered in Malawi at the hands of guerrilla fighters in Mozambique.

While in the refugee camps in Mozambique and studying their Bibles, many Witnesses came to believe in the biblical teaching that they were in the new covenant and were therefore going to heaven when they died. As a result, 500 Witnesses were disfellowshipped for this heresy on the charge of apostasy!

Nevertheless, many lost their lives, many were beaten, many were raped, and many had no possessions to return to, since they had been stolen or destroyed. All this for the sake of a 25-cent card which had nothing to do with neutrality!

The authors remember well how these waves of persecution were treated by Witnesses in other parts of the world. Magazine articles were emblazoned with shocking headlines in *The Watchtower* and *Awake!* Congregation meetings were devoted to discussion of the persecution and its obvious sign that Jehovah's

Witnesses, the "true" Christians, were being persecuted as foretold. Malawi became a rallying cry and a sign of God's approval. Witnesses were encouraged to write letters of protest to the country's President. A "circle the wagons" mentality prevailed and a solidarity resulted. This became a confirmation of the 1975 "end-of-the-world" prediction. The tragedy was exploited by the Watch Tower organization. The African Witnesses were the sacrifice. Since 1977 there have been no statistical reports on Malawi in the Society's annual yearbook. There is nothing to report.

In November of 1986 a special four-page insert was passed out to Jehovah's Witnesses at their weekly service/sales meeting. It was from the Governing Body of Jehovah's Witnesses. The document outlined in detail the events that are unfolding in another country of Africa—Rwanda. Once again African Witnesses are suffering persecution over what is essentially the same issue as what occurred in Malawi! As in Malawi, Rwanda has one political party and in recent years a minimum contribution of 100 Rwandese Francs (approximately one U.S. dollar) has been required of all party members. The Rwandese are automatically considered members of the party when they reach the age of 18, so it is not a matter of joining anything.

If this appears shocking to the reader, what follows should prove to be beyond comprehension, for the life-and-death choices that Witnesses are forced to make are not the same for all Jehovah's Witnesses.

In the country of Mexico it is necessary for men of draft age to submit to a period of military training lasting one year. Each man registers and receives a certificate or "cartilla." He is supposed to attend weekly military instruction, and his "cartilla" is duly noted by an official. Although it is illegal for an official to fill in the certificate if in fact the registrant has not attended, it is a common practice. Officials are regularly bribed by the Mexican men, including Mexican Jehovah's Witnesses!

This procedure has been condoned by the Governing Body of

Jehovah's Witnesses in spite of the fact that the issue of political/ military neutrality is involved. While the Witnesses in Malawi and now in Rwanda could have legally avoided their horrific experiences for what amounted to pennies in a closed one-party state, Mexican Witnesses can *bribe* officials to receive a certificate that states they are bona fide members of the Mexican military service.

The Scriptures do not condone partiality or bribery—"For the Lord your God is the God of gods and the Lord of lords, the great, the mighty, and the awesome God who does not show partiality, nor take a bribe" (Deuteronomy 10:17); "You shall not distort justice; you shall not be partial, and you shall not take a bribe" (Deuteronomy 16:19). Yet both prevail in the Watch Tower system.

Raymond Franz relates that in November 1978, he visited the Mexico Branch Office as a member of the Governing Body. During the course of his visit the Branch committee brought the "cartilla" bribery issue to his attention. They stated that many Mexican Witnesses were stricken in their conscience because they recognized that the issue was basically the same issue as that which had prevailed in Malawi. Franz was shown correspondence to prove that what was going on was in full accord with Watch Tower headquarters.

At the time of this writing, the double standard is still in effect.

The Watch Tower leadership wields total power over the lives of its followers. This includes matters of medical treatment that are considered normal by most persons.

The Watch Tower Society has a long history of unusual rules respecting medical and health practices. Early issues of *The Watchtower* magazine contained advertisements and brief articles on quack cures. Clayton J. Woodworth, a leading Bible Student and later editor of *The Golden Age* magazine, was a health faddist and a hater of the medical profession. Woodworth's eccentricities included denial of the American Medical Association. He also denied the germ theory of disease, which culminated in an all-out attack on smallpox vaccination beginning in the 1930's. These attitudes were reflected in his articles for the Society.

It was also during this period that individuals at Watch Tower headquarters, including Judge Rutherford, engaged in medical treatment called "radio diagnosis." It involved use of a machine called an oscilloclast, supposedly a diagnostic and healing machine. In reality it was nothing more than a black box consisting of an ohmmeter, rheostat, condenser, and other electrical gadgets wired together without rhyme or reason.[1]

A former Jehovah's Witness informed the authors that as late as 1957 some Witnesses were employing the use of these machines. In fact, this witness says he was cured of a cold in the office of a Jehovah's Witness chiropractor who used an "oscilloclast" for certain cases.

At the same time that this bizarre activity was going on, official Watch Tower publications were condemning smallpox vaccination as a crime, an outrage, and a delusion:

> Thinking people would rather have smallpox than vaccination, because the latter sows the seed of syphilis, cancers, eczema, erysipelas, scrofula, consumption, even leprosy and many other loathsome affections. Hence the practice of vaccination is a crime, an outrage and a delusion.[2]

Earlier in the same year of 1929 (when the above quotation was made), *The Golden Age*, published by the Watch Tower Bible and Tract Society, called the medical profession—

> . . . an institution founded on ignorance, error, and superstition. Some day so-called medical science will discover that all its "discoveries" have disclosed nothing but its own ignorance.[3]

By 1931 Jehovah's Witnesses were being told that vaccination was against God's law! This was based on a rigid interpretation of Genesis 9:4, when God told Noah, "You shall not eat flesh with its life, that is, its blood."

Watch Tower researcher Duane Magnani reports that during the more than 20 years that vaccination was "against God's law" for Jehovah's Witnesses, no less than 100 articles were written condemning the medical practice of vaccination. This caused problems for Jehovah's Witnesses when it became compulsory for children to be vaccinated and present a certificate to that effect when entering school. Also, persons leaving and reentering the country had to have these certificates.

Bill Cetnar was a longtime Jehovah's Witness who pioneered and eventually worked at Bethel headquarters in Brooklyn. He writes about how Jehovah's Witnesses broke the law to comply with "God's law."

> My wife's parents did what many other Witness parents were doctrinally constrained to do. They took her to a doctor who simulated a vaccination on her leg by the use of acid. He signed the certificate and she had no trouble getting into school. Joan's cousin also had a similar "vaccination," but unfortunately the doctor accidentally spilled the acid on her leg. She carries the scar to this day. I was told that A.E. Ilett, the Bethel doctor, filled out certificates without vaccinations. This must have been the case, because without vaccinations Witness missionaries could not leave the country and they got certificates somewhere.[4]

In 1952 "God's organization" changed its policy on vaccination. After more than two decades of controversy and heartache, the following change was presented:

> The matter of vaccination is one for the individual that has to face it to decide for himself. Each individual has to take the consequences for whatever position and

action he takes toward a case of compulsory vaccination, doing so according to his own conscience and his appreciation of what is for good health and the interests of advancing God's work. And our Society cannot afford to be drawn into the affair legally or take the responsibily for the way the case turns out.

After consideration of the matter, it does not appear to us to be in violation of the everlasting covenant made with Noah, as set down in Genesis 9:4, nor contrary to God's related commandment at Leviticus 17:10-14. . . . Hence all objection to vaccination on Scriptural grounds seems to be lacking.[5]

This now became a matter of conscience among the Witnesses, but many continued to feel that it was not advisable to receive vaccinations. Eight years after the ban was lifted, Emily Hood was exposed to this type of thinking. In a personal letter to us, Emily recounts her experience:

In 1960, after having been married for almost two years, I mentioned to Sister W., who had been studying with me for a year, that as soon as my husband returned from sea duty, we planned to start our family. She informed me that having a baby inoculated against diseases was the same as giving it a blood transfusion. By this time I had learned not to question the teachings of the Watch Tower Society. My daughter was 18 months old when she contacted pertussis (whooping cough) from Sister W.'s daughter. The next six weeks were very difficult and there were times when I thought Michelle might choke to death. During this time no Jehovah's Witnesses offered to help me in any way, but I was expected to continue with my Bible study. Sister W.'s son was born in January, 1963. A few months later, she and the Circuit Servant's wife and their babies dropped in for a visit. They told me they had just come from the Well-Baby Clinic, where they had had their children inoculated. I was in such shock I couldn't even ask why it was a law of Jehovah two years ago not to have vaccinations and now it wasn't. We were transferred out of that area less than a year later. I never did ask for an explanation. To this day I don't know if this was just one more way Sister W. had of controlling me or if she really didn't know the ban had been lifted eight years before. In any event, I never received an explanation nor an apology.

We wonder how many Jehovah's Witness children were submitting to acid burns or lying on beds of sickness because their parents did not want to break "God's law." This is the legacy that led to the ban on blood transfusions and also, for 13 years, the ban on organ transplants.

In the face of medical advances, the Watch Tower could not maintain such a hard line. By 1965 the following admission was made by the Society:

There can be little doubt that vaccinations appear to have caused a marked decrease in the number of people contracting certain contagious diseases. During the first thirty years of this century there were thousands of smallpox cases in the United States. From 1920 to 1930 alone, they ran from 30,000 to 100,000 annually, but in recent years there have been only about 55 cases of smallpox annually, with no deaths. Vaccinations also appear to have caused a decline in polio.[6]

Cannibalism

In 1967 Jehovah's Witnesses were once again admonished to stay clear of accepted medical practice in the case of organ transplants. Prior to that time the Society had commented in a general way concerning transplants. Now the organization informed the Witnesses that transplants were *cannibalism*! The issue was addressed in the November 15, 1967, *Watchtower*, on pages 702-704, when a reader asked, "Is there any scriptural objection to donating one's body for use in medical research or to accepting organs for transplant from such a source?"

An extended answer followed, but the following was the heart of the message:

> Those who submit to such operations are thus living off the flesh of another human. That is cannibalistic. . . . Jehovah God did not grant permission for humans to try to perpetuate their lives by cannibalistically taking into their bodies human flesh, whether chewed or in the form of whole organs or body parts taken from others.

In effect, then, the "faithful and discreet slave" closed the door on organ transplants. In a *Detroit Free Press* interview at that time, Watch Tower official Milton G. Henschel stated: "Transplanting organs is really cannibalism. . . . In transplants, you are taking something from another body to sustain your life. . . . If a person gains another five years, because of a transplant, what has he gained, if he loses the future?"

Continuously through the 1970's, numerous articles were developed showing the inadvisability of transplants and the dire results from such a practice. Then in 1980 the Society reversed itself. In another "Questions from Readers" article in the March 15, 1980, *Watchtower*, on page 31, a reader asked if a congregation should exercise disciplinary action against a baptized member that accepts a human organ transplant. In part, this was the response:

> It may be argued, too, that organ transplants are different from cannibalism since the "donor" is not

killed to supply food. . . . While the Bible specifically
forbids consuming blood, there is no Biblical command pointedly forbidding the taking in of other human tissue. For this reason, each individual faced with
making a decision on this matter should carefully and
prayerfully weigh matters and then decide conscientiously what he or she could or could not do before
God.

The conclusion was that the congregation judicial committee
should not take any action if someone accepted an organ transplant. It could be asked, during the 13 years from 1967 to 1980,
how many Witnesses or their children went blind without a
cornea transplant. How many died rather than accept an organ
transplant? Or on the other hand, how many were disfellowshipped for having an organ transplant? What tragedies occurred
before the "faithful and discreet slave" changed its mind?

"Ye Are Not to Eat the Blood"

Of all the peculiar medical beliefs held by Jehovah's Witnesses, none is more deeply entrenched or has endured as long as
that of abstaining from blood transfusions. This practice has
exceeded all the other medical oddities practiced by Witnesses,
both in the number of lives lost over the issue and the controversy
connected with it.

As early as 1892, Russell knew that the eating of blood was
prohibited to the Jews and continued as counsel to the early
Christians (for example, in Acts 15:19,20) in order to avoid
offending Jewish Christians. This was developed in the November 15, 1892, issue of *Zion's Watch Tower*. Russell, in agreement
with Christian commentaries on the subject, showed that this
suggested abstinence was to guard against the Gentile Christians
becoming stumbling blocks to Jewish Christians. He reminded
his readers that this command had been given earlier to Noah, in
Genesis 9:4.

Today the Watch Tower leaders ignore this article written by the first President. Rather, they point to an article written in the December 15, 1927, issue of *The Watchtower* as evidence that as early as 1927 the Society recognized the error of transfusion as well as the eating of blood.[7] This is nonsensical because the mention of the eating of blood was a small aside thrown into an article entitled "One Reason for God's Vengeance." The article was devoted to the subject of murder, both of humans and the wanton killing of animals for sport. In the seven long pages of discussion, the following innocuous statement was introduced because it was part of a verse under discussion:

> God told Noah that every living creature should be meat unto him; but that he must not eat the blood, because the life is in the blood.[8]

In 1939 President Rutherford answered a letter in *The Watchtower* asking about the advisability of eating clean or unclean animals (i.e. pork). Apparently the writer of the letter was in a quandary about the covenant of Noah and the covenant of the law and their applications to Christians. Rutherford stated within the framework of his answer:

> The weight of all the argument about these texts is that the life is in the blood and that the blood must not be eaten. That would be true of a clean animal or an unclean one just the same . . . and if an animal is killed and the blood not poured out, but eaten, then the man who does it is guilty of death, for the reason that no man shall drink blood without dying.[9]

This made it very clear to any Witness that might not understand the Watch Tower's teaching on eating blood. Interestingly, at this time Jehovah's Witnesses accepted blood transfusions. The first time blood transfusion was condemned was in the December 22, 1943, *Consolation* magazine. This particular article concerned an experiment in connection with the use of horse blood. The article also took a swipe at immunization. The article summed up on page 23: "The divine prohibition as to eating or partaking of blood does not appear to trouble the 'scientists.' "

In *The Watchtower* magazine of December 1, 1944, an article entitled "The Stranger's Right Maintained" was written concerning the strangers or alien residents in ancient Israel and their modern counterparts. This laborious ten-page article went into types and antitypes concerning these matters. However, a new thought was woven into the article in a clever way. On page 362 the following statement was made:

> Not only as a descendant of Noah, but now also as one bound by God's law to Israel which incorporated the everlasting covenant regarding the sanctity of life-sustaining blood, the stranger was forbidden to eat or drink blood, whether by transfusion or by the mouth (Gen. 9:4; Lev. 17:10-14).

Neither Genesis 9:4 nor Leviticus 17:10-14 even hint at transfusion within their rendering. Yet the thought was now introduced that transfusions broke God's law. This attempt to show the antiquity of transfusion and the prohibition of it is nothing short of ridiculous. Both Genesis and Leviticus were written thousands of years before the practice of transfusion.

The Society tied transfusion to right and wrong worship in an article entitled "Immovable For The Right Worship" in the July 1, 1945, *Watchtower*. Partway through the article they mentioned the importance of keeping free from blood and cited examples of early transfusion cases, including the first reported transfusion experiment in 1492 A.D. This article did not openly prohibit transfusions. However, it associated transfusion with eating or drinking blood. While the article did not directly forbid blood transfusion, by this time many Witnesses were becoming increasingly aware of the transfusion problem.

By 1948 it was becoming very clear how the Witnesses viewed blood transfusion:

> According to God's law, humans are not to take into their system the blood of others. "Whatsoever soul it be that eateth any manner of blood, even that soul shall be cut off from his people." "Thou shalt not eat it; that it may go well with thee, and with thy children after thee." (Leviticus 7:27; Deuteronomy 12:25) In addition to the danger of disobeying God's law, blood transfusion involves health hazards.[10]

The Watch Tower organization was obviously conditioning and preparing Witnesses for an out-and-out prohibition against blood transfusions. Things had come a long way from the condemnation of eating blood in the 1927 *Watchtower* to the denouncement of blood transfusion in the 1948 *Awake!*

Matters came to a head in 1951. The "Questions From Readers" section in the July 1, 1951, *Watchtower* magazine referred to a Chicago court case in which the stand of Jehovah's Witnesses concerning blood transfusions received wide publicity.

The case involved Rhoda and Darrell Labrenz and their six-day-old baby Cheryl. The child had a rare blood condition in which the red cells were being destroyed. Her parents refused to allow a blood transfusion for the child and the court in Chicago charged them with technical neglect. The baby was removed from their custody and was given the necessary transfusion in order to save her life.

The story was reported in the May 22, 1951, issue of *Awake!* Rhoda Labrenz was quoted as saying that, much as she wanted a little girl, "We can't break Jehovah's law."

Nine questions were raised and the *Watchtower* answers followed. The answers to the questions laid out in no uncertain terms that it was not permissible for Witnesses to take blood transfusions. The article said in part on page 415:

Any saving of life accomplished by transfusions is short-lived. And doing it in disobedience of God's commands could cost one eternal life. No temporary good done could justify this permanent great loss.

Many more sensational cases and examples followed, and the Witness stand on blood transfusions frequently became headline news. In the *Awake!* story about the Labrenz case, a statement was made that in essence has become a credo among Jehovah's Witnesses with respect to the blood transfusion issue:

Those who die faithful to God will be resurrected to live eternally in that new earth arrangement, whereas those who break His laws will perish and never be resurrected. So it was with this farsighted view of possibilities of eternal life in mind that Rhoda Labrenz said what she did. The Scriptures show that in divine judgment periods such as our day babes share the fate of their parents, either for good or for bad. Faithful parents open the way to life for their as yet unresponsible offspring. Stated bluntly, better to die now maintaining integrity and later be resurrected than to compromise now and live for a brief time, only to be dead forever later on.[11]

At this time, although it was supposedly up to the conscience of the individual Witness, if he decided to take a transfusion he was more or less ostracized. This would soon change. "God's law" was not to be broken, and it became a disfellowshipping offense in 1961.

In addition, in the September 15, 1961, *Watchtower* it was revealed that Witnesses were not to use any blood fractions or components of blood. Page 558:

Is God's law violated by such medical use of blood? Is it wrong to sustain life by infusions of blood or plasma or red cells or the various blood fractions? Yes! The law that God gave to Noah and which applies to all his descendants makes it wrong for anyone to eat blood, that is, to use the blood of another creature to nourish or sustain one's life.

The article went to great length to explain that Witnesses should check the ingredients of products they purchased to see if there were any blood by-products or blood itself used in them. This included wieners, bologna, cold cuts, meat loaves, hamburger, plasma powder in pastry, tonics, and tablets of various kinds. Witnesses were to check if chickens they bought had been properly bled. In some lands they had to all but abandon ordering a meat dinner in restaurants. Eventually they even became cautious as to the plywood they bought, because it became known that some manufacturers used plasma in the glue that held it together. It seems incredible that the Scriptures concerning the eating of blood could include plywood! The authors remember well the almost-frenzied state that prevailed among the congregations. Blood transfusions and blood products became a preoccupation that almost exceeded the interest in the end of the world.

The issue of transfusions created an obvious problem for Jehovah's Witness hemophiliacs, for they were not permitted to receive the clotting factor necessary to control fatal bleeding. The Watch Tower leaders were emphatic that blood fractions could not be used. [12] However, by 1978 this became a "gray area" and serum injections made from blood derivatives became a matter of conscience. *The Watchtower* of June 15, 1978, on pages 30 and 31, stated in part:

What, however, about accepting serum injections to fight against disease, such as are employed for diphtheria, tetanus, viral hepatitis, rabies, hemophilia and Rh incompatibility? This seems to fall into a "gray area." Some Christians believe that accepting a small amount of a blood derivative for such a purpose would not be a manifestation of disrespect for God's law; their conscience would permit such. (Compare Luke 6:1-5.) Others, though, feel conscientiously obliged to refuse serums because these contain blood, though only a tiny amount. Hence, we have taken the position that this question must be resolved by each individual on a personal basis. We urge each one to strive to have a clear conscience and to be responsive to God's guidance found in His Word.

The reader will notice the innocuous mention of "hemophilia" in the quotation. This triggered quite a response from Witness hemophiliacs because, unlike serum injections used to combat the diseases mentioned, hemophiliacs require ongoing infusions of blood fractions to control against fatal bleeding. Many hemophiliacs receive as many as 30 to 50 infusions of Factor VIII a year, according to the National Hemophilia Foundation. A single injection of the blood concentrate called Factor VIII may contain proteins from as many as 2500 donors. Thus a hemophiliac may receive Factor VIII from 25,000 to 75,000 donors a year.

Another interesting point involving a principle is involved. Should a Jehovah's Witness hemophiliac decide to take all the necessary injections to sustain his life, as many as 75,000 persons may have donated blood so that he might live. However, Jehovah's Witnesses cannot return that gesture of love and concern by donating blood so that some other hemophiliac may live. Should a Jehovah's Witness hemophiliac decide to go the whole way and take as many injections as needed to sustain life, can it be said that he is abstaining from blood, due to the large volume of blood needed to treat hemophiliacs?

Many Witness hemophiliacs do not take Factor VIII because of conscience. Others take repeated infusions of this blood clotting agent. Some have only taken one infusion because they are not aware that the policy has changed. How many have died over this divided and double standard? Indeed, how many sincere Witnesses have died down through the years because of not taking a needed blood transfusion because "God's organization" has decreed that this is against His law?

Watch Tower leaders appear to have once again decided to tighten up on Jehovah's Witness hemophiliacs receiving Factor VIII transfusions. In the June 22, 1987, *Awake!* an article written by a Witness hemophiliac relates how he has survived without a transfusion from 1970 to the present. The strong implication is that to do otherwise would be "a breaking of integrity to God." An article such as this probes the conscience of other Witness hemophiliacs with the thought that they are breaking their integrity by taking Factor VIII transfusions. It also carries the strength and tacit policy of the Governing Body, who approved the article for publication.

The really important question is: Do Jehovah's Witnesses refuse blood on scriptural grounds or because the Watch Tower organization tells them to? We believe that if the organization published a different interpretation of the Bible verses which they use in support of their stand on blood, Jehovah's Witnesses would agree to take blood transfusions without any hesitation. Why do we say this? Because as soon as the Watch Tower leadership reversed its teaching on vaccination, organ transplants, and blood serums and fractions, thousands of Witnesses abandoned their conscientious refusal. They were really following the changeable Watch Tower organization's instructions rather than the Scriptures, which never change.

A thought-provoking statement is made in the 1977 Society publication *Jehovah's Witnesses and the Question of Blood*, page 41:

> Consequently, whether having religious objections to blood transfusions or not many a person might decline blood simply because it is essentially an organ transplant that at best is only partially compatible with his own blood.

If blood is essentially an organ transplant, and organ transplants are now permissible for Jehovah's Witnesses, does it follow that perhaps the Governing Body will eventually change their rules on blood transfusion? Unfortunately, we feel they will not. They have dug themselves into a deep hole with this teaching. The Watch Tower leadership will never directly say that taking blood is up to the individual's conscience, because of the serious reaction they would receive from members who have let a loved one die. Parents would realize that their children had died needlessly and might be tempted to storm the doors of Watchtower headquarters.

Instead, people continue to suffer needlessly because of this cruel policy. In the following chapter we want to tell the story of a family who suffered needlessly for the cause.

13
Jenny

Paul and Pat Blizard had two boys and longed for a girl. So it was with great joy that Jenny Leigh Blizard was born on August 10, 1980. However, the ecstasy was short-lived. Five weeks after Jenny's birth, Pat was trimming the baby's fingernails and accidentally nicked her finger. It would not stop bleeding.

The Blizards rushed their child to the doctor and were informed that something was seriously wrong: Jenny's blood would not clot. The doctor sent them to specialists in San Angelo, Texas, about 100 miles away.

During this time bruises began to appear on Jenny's chest and back. She was hemorrhaging internally. The doctors in San Angelo were afraid to take blood out of her arm for tests for fear that she might bleed to death. As they did not have equipment or facilities for this rare case, it was arranged for the Blizards to take Jenny to the Santa Rosa Medical Center's special care nursery in San Antonio, about 150 miles away. There the doctors spent five days trying to analyze why little Jenny's blood would not clot. Finally they concluded that she had a rare liver disease—biliary atresia.

By now the doctors were trying desperately to save Jenny's life. "We know you are Jehovah's Witnesses," said one of the specialists. "We know you're not supposed to take blood, that it's against your religion. But you have to make a decision. We don't want an explanation about your doctrine. We just want a yes or no answer. Will you let us give your daughter a transfusion?"

It is difficult to typify the life of a Jehovah's Witness. Although there are many things common to them all—rules, regulations, meeting attendance, door-to-door peddling, and isolation from the larger community—individual circumstances and the vicissitudes of life vary with individuals. Some are born into the faith and remain all their lives with never a doubt. Others are drawn into it as converts and also remain in it the remainder of their lives. Many others question, investigate the facts, and leave. Some tire of waiting for Armageddon and just drift away, remaining tacit Jehovah's Witnesses although no longer participants in the movement. Some would welcome a chance to test their commitment. A few, however, must face the ultimate test of their faith.

That is the predicament that confronted Paul and Pat. Their story contains many of the elements that make up the life and aspirations of the average Witness. But it has a cruel twist that goes beyond the experience encountered by most Jehovah's Witnesses.

Paul remembers that as a boy he was never encouraged to use his mind. As his family continually moved all over the country to serve the Watchtower organization, he attended 12 schools in 12 years. As a boy, Paul was interested in a musical or artistic career. However, his parents always reminded him, "Wait until the new world. Then we'll have time to develop those talents."

When he was a senior in high school, the circuit overseer advised Paul to quit school and go into full-time pioneer work. It was 1971 and the world was going to end in 1975. Paul heeded the advice and pioneered full-time for two years. "I was really zealous at what I did," he says today. "In fact, some of the Witnesses thought I was too zealous even as a Witness. I would stand out in front of churches and pass out *Watchtowers* and warn people that Armageddon was going to strike in 1975. I had one preacher tell me, 'Will you come to my office on January 1, 1976, and visit with me?' I said, 'Sure! You're not going to be here!' I was so cocky. I was so sure that was the truth."

In 1973 Paul was invited by President Knorr to work a three-year term at the Watch Tower world headquarters in Brooklyn,

New York. He considered this an honor and privilege. Since he couldn't go to college, he figured this would be the best education he could receive. He soon realized that his education was little more than slave labor (at the time, the stipend for members of the Bethel family was just 14 dollars per month).

Shortly after he arrived, he entered an elevator in which the operator asked him how long he had been in Bethel. When Paul replied, "one week," the operator said, "If I had that long to go, I'd put a rock around my neck and jump off the Brooklyn Bridge." Paul later told us reflectively, "There were times I wanted to, I guarantee you."

Paul was assigned to work in the shipping department and stayed there about a year. Then he was moved into the bindery, where he worked the night shift. Everybody dreaded an assignment in the bindery because the work was so tedious. Paul had to feed books into machines one at a time for hours on end. He says he averaged over 19,000 books per night, feeding them into machines one at a time. "It was very boring and you didn't have any say over where you would work the next week or the next year," Paul says. "They would just come up to you and say, 'Now it's God's will that we're going to move you to another job.' If you protested you were rebelling against God's organization and were subject to disciplinary action."

Paul learned some unexpected skills at the Watch Tower headquarters. For example, a well-entrenched spy system exists at Bethel. Persons would turn each other in for various offenses. In spite of this spy system, there was an inordinate amount of drinking. Paul said, "I learned to drink at Bethel. If you are not a drinking man when you go there, you are when you leave." When Paul returned home, his mother found a quart of Jack Daniels whiskey in his suitcase. She asked him, "Is this what you learn at Bethel?" His reply was, "No, but it helps."

Paul and Patricia had a long-distance courtship and then married in June 1976, after Paul completed his term at Bethel. Pat had been a pioneer and special pioneer missionary for eight years. Under the direction of the Watch Tower Society in New York, she was sent to different parts of the United States. Like Paul, she had dedicated her life to serving God.

Persons who have served at headquarters are considered worthy of greater responsibilities in local congregations. Paul was used extensively by the elders in his congregation. Paul explained what some of these responsibilities included: "... training in some of the 'undercover' work of the elders. It was exciting to follow members of the congregation around at night who were suspected of wrongdoing. We used binoculars sometimes. I was also given access to the congregation files, which revealed the inside information of everyone in the congregation. I was being used in covert operations that I had so graphically seen control the workers at headquarters."

About this time a friend introduced Paul to a book, *Thirty Years a Watchtower Slave*, written by a former Jehovah's Witness, William Schnell. Since it is forbidden to read any anti-Watchtower material, Paul knew that it was his duty to turn his friend in to the elders for a judicial hearing. Instead he decided to read the book.

The contents of the book were very disturbing. The author was a former worker at headquarters, and Paul could relate to many of the things that he was exposing. "Things that I had tried to erase from my memory were surfacing again, and questions of the Watch Tower's authority left me very unsettled. The author mentioned that he had found the truth from studying the Bible apart from the Watchtower publications."

As a result of that book, Paul and Pat decided to purchase a New American Standard Bible to study, rather than the Watch Tower's New World Translation. They secretly studied their new Bible long hours into the night. They also read some of the older publications of the Society from the Russell and Rutherford eras. They discovered that many of the major doctrines that they were willing to die for were false and also that the Society was guilty of many outrageous prophecies, all of which had failed.

Paul confronted his father—an elder in the congregation—
about some of these issues. Since Paul was questioning Watchtower teachings, his father reported his son and daughter-in-law
to the elders. The couple was forced to stand trial for apostasy.
"After a lengthy hearing with many tears, we repented for doubting the Watch Tower Society and were allowed to remain as
Witnesses. But I was stripped of all my responsibilities in
the congregation. I was to be watched for a period of time before being allowed to serve in any capacity in the congregation
again."

A welcome relief came when a job transfer took the Blizards to
Brady, Texas. Paul looked forward to a fresh start, but under the
Watch Tower system this was not possible. The judicial hearing
from the previous congregation was now part of Paul's permanent file. The elders in the new congregation informed Paul that
they would be watching him for a period of time to see if these
apostate ideas of his would resurface. They warned him that they
would disfellowship him if he tried to share such ideas with
anyone else in the congregation. Paul vowed loyalty to the organization, and said he would not read or speak about anything that
differed from the Watch Tower's explanation of Scripture.

Two years passed. Paul reports: "Being under the close scru-
tiny of the elders left me empty. Nothing and no one, not even my
children, who had brought me so much joy, made my life fulfilling. We needed something, but what it was we did not know. My
wife and I would drink to excess often, searching for some kind of
joy. But only emptiness resulted."

Then little Jenny was born, and life began to look bright
again—until their daughter wound up in San Antonio, fighting
for her life. The doctor looked Paul straight in the eye and said:
"Mr. and Mrs. Blizard, you have to make a decision—yes or no—
whether your child lives or dies."

The couple was devastated. Paul admits today that while he
was aware of the blood issue, he never thought he would have to
face that choice. The couple asked the doctors to leave the room.
They needed a few minutes to pray before making their decision.

Paul picked up his precious daughter, who was connected to wires and machines that kept her alive. "I started to weep," he says. "We prayed and held hands together and I said 'Oh God, Jehovah, what kind of a God are You to force us to make a decision about whether Jenny lives or dies?"

Patricia continues, "We prayed about it, and thought about everything we had been taught. We had a real distinct impression that we were supposed to obey God's law. We were to let our daughter die. So we called the doctors back in and told them."

Within 15 minutes the hospital officials had contacted the Texas Child Welfare Department and a suit was filed against the Blizards for child abuse and neglect. A court order was issued to insure that Jenny would receive the blood needed to save her life. Half an hour later, a sheriff's deputy came in and issued citations to the couple. The deputy also warned the hospital staff not to allow the Blizards to remove Jenny from the hospital. This warning was not unusual—Jehovah's Witnesses have a history of sneaking persons out of hospitals to avoid blood transfusions.

Somehow word spread quickly throughout the Witness community. There was a four-hour span between the issuance of the court order and the transfusion while the doctors matched up Jenny's blood type. During this period Witnesses, strangers to the Blizards, came up and swarmed the room, waving *Watchtower* articles and stating: "You can't let your child take that blood." One Witness said to them, "If she dies, you'll get her back in the resurrection. So all hope isn't lost." That wasn't very comforting to Paul and Pat.

Then a group of elders arrived, took Paul off to one side, and asked, "Has your daughter gotten the blood yet?" When Paul replied that the hospital staff were still matching the blood, an elder said, "Great, we still have time to get her out of the hospital. We can sneak her out in the middle of the night. We can hire a helicopter. Just unhook the tubes and we're gone."

Paul answered, "Wait a minute—you can't do that. It's against the law. I'm under court order. I would be charged with murder."

The elder said, "That's a chance you're going to have to take. You must obey God rather than men."

"Look, I just can't let my child die in that way," Paul appealed. "We have made the decision that we would not give our permission for her to receive a transfusion. We are willing to let her die. But you can't force me to take her out. That would kill her for sure. I just can't do it."

As the angry elders left, one of them said, "I hope your daughter gets hepatitis from that blood." That was the final straw for Paul. Here were his own people, God's organization, turning against him and cursing him because he wanted to see his child live. Now he and his wife were all alone, with no emotional support.

The necessary blood transfusion was administered to Jenny. Two San Antonio newspapers picked up the story and reported the case. As a result, local Witnesses came to the hospital room and commended the Blizards for their faithful stand—that is, until they learned that the Blizards had refused to break the law and risk Jenny's life by sneaking her out of the hospital. The Witnesses then left the room in contempt.

When they returned home to Brady with Jenny, the Blizards discovered the effect that Jenny's transfusion had on their congregation. Although Paul and Pat could not be disfellowshipped because they had not freely allowed the transfusion, nevertheless they were shunned as outcasts. Little Jenny was treated as if she were contaminated, or as Paul said, "like a leper."

A few weeks later it was decided that Jenny would require exploratory surgery. As the court order was about to run out, Paul and Pat wanted the operation done without further blood transfusions. They located a doctor in Houston who agreed to do the surgery without blood.

Patricia took Jenny to Houston for the operation and stayed there for a week. Paul could not accompany her as he had to keep working to pay for the mounting expenses. While alone in Houston, a Witness family with whom Pat had stayed during her pioneer days was kind to her. They gave her 100 dollars and had their two daughters stay with her during the surgery. The surgery was successful, with no blood used, and Pat returned to Brady with Jenny. It was the last loving act they experienced from a Witness family.

If Ye Have Love Among Yourselves

Jenny required constant care and had to be taken to the doctor regularly. Nights were especially hard because the baby woke up frequently. Paul would take his turns at night but could not help much beyond that. He was now working 16-hour days to try to pay for the expensive medication and food supplements that Jenny required.

The Blizards' boys were aged two and three respectively, and needed supervision when Pat took Jenny to the doctor. Pat asked two of her Witness friends if they would babysit the boys on these occasions. They were reluctant and did so begrudgingly. They were even more hesitant when Pat asked them to mind the boys all day when it became necessay to take Jenny regularly to a clinic in San Angelo, a distance of 85 miles each way. It became increasingly apparent that the Witness community was rejecting them. Members of the local Kingdom Hall did not come over and visit or offer assistance. Paul states: "My own parents wouldn't help us out. We were rejects because we had not prevented Jenny from taking the blood."

At eight months Jenny contracted a stomach virus and became seriously dehydrated. Once again Pat Blizard had to take her daughter to the hospital in San Angelo. She spent a week alone there with Jenny, who required intravenous feeding. Pat was up night and day for most of the time, yet received no help from the organization she had faithfully served for so many years. She called Paul's father, and he said he would contact the local congregation in San Angelo to get her some assistance. None was forthcoming. She did not receive one phone call or visit during the week.

Fortunately, a Christian lady from the department of human resources brought Pat a basket of fruit and a book of inspirational sayings about God. This kind lady asked Pat if she needed anything else and attended to her. After Pat returned home to Brady, she called this lady and asked if there was any way they could get some financial help. The medical bills continued to mount, with Jenny needing special formula and medicine. Paul's job just could not keep up with the added expenses.

The lady asked what church Pat attended and the pastor's name. After getting the number of the local Kingdom Hall, she contacted one of the congregation elders, informed him of the financial need within the Blizard family, and asked if the congregation could help. The elder's response was succinct: "We don't have any arrangement like that." With that, the resourceful lady contacted some of the churches in Brady.

The response was immediate and overwhelming. Without questioning the Blizard's beliefs, donations came in from the churches and individuals. A ladies' sorority opened a bank account with a contribution of 500 dollars to help with Jenny's medication and travel expenses back and forth to San Angelo. They kept adding to this in the years to come. The Baptist young women's mission group offered to help in any way they could, which included babysitting the boys during the frequent trips to the doctors, as well as giving Pat a much-needed break. Neighbors and complete strangers brought meals and food as well as offers of money to help Jenny.

The help and understanding from the people of Brady gave Paul and Pat a new perspective about Jehovah's Witnesses. It provided an opportunity for this young couple to see living Christianity in action—not just by word but also by deed. Pat relates that her first thought was not "Why are these people helping me and the Witnesses are not?" but rather "I can't believe that Jehovah will destroy these people at Armageddon."

Paul recounts: "We had always been taught that the only ones who show love are God's organization, Jehovah's Witnesses. Yet these people were loving us and showing care. I said to my wife, 'Something is definitely wrong here. These people aren't even

Christians—we believed we were the only true Christians—and yet they are showing Christian love and our own brothers, God's organization, won't have anything to do with us.' That really shook us, to the point where we started investigating and studying the Bible again."

The Blizards wanted to talk about their confusion. But to whom? They had been taught never to trust preachers; they were anti-Christ. Yet these very people had been so loving. One of Paul's customers convinced him there was a preacher who would help him. Paul met the man and began to secretly study and discuss Scripture with him. Paul swore the minister, Pastor Ray Ash, to secrecy. During this time the Blizards attended church, and many of the cardinal doctrines that they had held dear all their lives began crumbling. Still, they warred with their consciences.

One weekend, while strolling at a mall, they passed a Christian bookstore. Paul said to Pat, "We've committed all these other sins; we might as well go in this Christian bookstore and look around. There they poured their hearts to the lady behind the counter. They told her that they were Jehovah's Witnesses, but were doubting. Everything they believed they were finding to be false when they read the Bible.

The lady in the store shared the plan of salvation with the Blizards. On their way home the couple held hands and prayed a simple prayer of surrender to Jesus. Paul remembers thinking that they were giving up everything—their family, their way of life— for this. "But actually we gave up nothing and gained everything, because at that very moment, when we prayed that prayer, we felt a release, a freedom. When we got home we picked up our Bible and all the questions we had about our salvation, about who we were, were answered. We were born again. We were Christians. We were new creatures in Christ. It wasn't something that we had to work for anymore. All the thousands of hours that we put in for an organization—it was finished. We experienced a joy that we never had as Witnesses."

Aftermath

Shortly thereafter Paul and Pat Blizard joined the Baptist church they had attended. It so happened that the service when they went forward for membership was on local radio. Later that day a Witness lady came by to visit. After some small talk, she remarked that there was a ridiculous rumor circulating that Paul and Pat had joined the Baptist church. When Pat confirmed that this was so, the Witness lady quickly excused herself, stating that she had to go and make some calls.

That night the Blizards received a call from the elders ordering them to appear at a committee meeting, which of course would have been for the express purpose of disfellowshipping them. Pastor Ash happened to come by right after that call and observed Paul's agitation. "What's the problem, Paul?" he asked.

"I'm worried about this meeting we're going to have with the elders," Paul replied.

"I've got a suggestion," said the pastor. "Why don't you just call them back and tell them you're not coming?"

Today Paul reflects, "I was so in tune with the control of Jehovah's Witnesses that I figured this was just the way it had to be. I had to submit to them and listen to them. Then I said, 'Hey, I am free now. I can just call them back and tell them I'm not coming.' And I did. They were shocked, and responded, 'You have got to be here.' I replied, 'I don't have to be anywhere. I'm a born-again, washed-in-the-blood child of the King, and I don't have to answer to any man.' The elder asked me if I had joined the church, and I said 'Amen' and hung up the phone."

Of course, the Blizards were disfellowshipped. Paul's father called Paul's relatives and friends all over the country to warn them that Paul and Pat were apostates, and not to have any contact with them. The wheels of the Watch Tower organization were in motion. Pat's parents, 1900 miles away, were immediately alerted and all contact was curtailed. The Blizard's parents, brothers, and sisters, as well as friends and associates, no longer acknowledged them, not even extending family courtesies.

The rejection they had felt as a result of Jenny's transfusion now turned to shunning by edict. Under threat of disfellowship-ment themselves, Jehovah's Witnesses, including blood relatives, could no longer have anything to do with the Blizards.

The cutoff was so extreme that Pat learned of her grand-mother's death six months later—from another relative who was not a Jehovah's Witnesses. Her mother didn't even write or call or tell her the news. Then a year later Pat's grandfather on the other side died. Pat had written her mother in between and asked to be informed of such news. But again, there was no contact from her family.

A number of years passed, and Paul and Pat continued to grow in their Christian walk. Paul worked part-time and attended college to further his education in preparation for full-time Christian ministry. Pat mothered little Jenny and their two boys, and in time another little girl was born to them. They gained as many Christian friends as they had lost among Jehovah's Wit-nesses. Although their relatives and parents would no longer have anything to do with them, not even to visit the children, the Blizards were sustained by their relationship with Christ.

Then once again tragedy struck. In January of 1987, Jenny, who was now six years old, became seriously ill. The doctor came to their home and diagnosed a peritonitis infection. Jenny was in heart failure by the time the ambulance came. At the hospital they removed fluid from Jenny's stomach and put her on antibiotics. She was hooked up to intravenous and put on oxygen in preparation for an emergency ambulance run to a Dallas hospital.

Patricia called her mother to tell her of Jenny's grave condi-tion. Her mother cried on the phone, saying, "I wish I could be there to help." Although she had never seen Jenny in all her six years of life, thereby maintaining loyalty to Watch Tower rules, her natural instincts as a mother showed. Pat's mother called Carol, Pat's sister, and they called to say, "Even though we believe differently than you do, we love you guys. And we miss you." They were kind words, and the first contact of any kind from either side of the family.

Although Jenny tenaciously held on to life, she was in a battle she could not win. On March 3, 1987, Jenny died. Paul and Pat had spent 39 days in a bedside vigil. They retired to a small motel in a nearby town and called the necessary people. Paul's parents had not contacted them during all the time at the hospital, even though they lived less than 50 miles away and knew of the crisis.

At the funeral service, members of the Blizard's church were there, as well as hundreds of persons from the surrounding area. Absent were any of the relatives of Paul and Pat Blizard. The couple sat by themselves in the section reserved for family, with empty chairs surrounding them. The same scenario unfolded at the gravesite, with Paul and Pat and their young sons the only ones in the family seating area. After the gravesite ceremony was completed, Pat's sister and brother-in-law appeared and went back to the Blizard's home for a brief visit.

And so it was that on March 6, 1987, Jenny Leigh Blizard was buried at Greenleaf Cemetery in Brownwood, Texas. She never knew her grandparents or other relatives in her brief six years of life. The rules of the Watch Tower organization were not broken.

Jenny's little tombstone simply says GOD'S SPECIAL MESSENGER. We pray that she was, for in her short life Christ's rule for true Christianity was put to the test: "By this shall all men know that ye are my disciples, if ye have love one to another" (John 13:35 KJV).

14

The Exodus

Before Mary Welch ever came into contact with Jehovah's Witnesses, she had a deep desire to know God. In 1968, at the age of 21, she began her search. At first she focused on various Eastern religions, but rejected them because they did not include Jesus Christ. Then she thought about reading the Bible, but that idea frightened her, for she had never opened a Bible and had only been in a church once in her life. She knew she would need someone to help her understand this mysterious book.

It was through her job as a hairdresser that she made a breakthrough. One of her customers was a Jehovah's Witness, and this woman seemed to understand the Bible. The woman offered to help Mary in her study of the Bible. The study lasted two years, and Mary was baptized in 1970. But the more she studied, the more confused she became. "I began to wonder why we were always told to witness about Jehovah and His kingdom when Jesus said, 'You will be witnesses of me,' " she says.[1] She also couldn't understand why she was taught that only 144,000 people would go to heaven when Revelation 7:9 says there would be an innumerable multitude standing before the throne. Nevertheless, she accepted the organization's teaching and authority.

Still, nagging questions cropped up in her mind. In 1973 the Society published information regarding proper sexual relations between husband and wife. It caused problems for some couples, particularly when one spouse was not a Witness. Mary noted how one couple was disfellowshipped over this issue. Then in 1978 the Society reversed its position. Mary wondered how an organization supposedly guided by God's Holy Spirit could make such a mistake. She asked her elders about this, but they gave her no answer. She wondered how many broken marriages occurred because of this wrong information. And this caused her to begin checking into previous issues and prophecies of the Watchtower over the past hundred years.

She finally concluded that the organization did not have the truth. During this period she was going through some serious health problems and depression following the birth of her second child. Yet her Witness friends never bothered to call and see if she needed help. She began to wonder what other religions believe, and embarked again on a search. In the process she read a book of testimonies by former Jehovah's Witnesses. One of the ex-Witnesses told how she had put her faith in the Lord Jesus Christ and asked Him to come into her life. "At last I realized that my salvation didn't depend on the Watchtower organization, but on Jesus Christ!" Mary says. "I finally realized that it is a gift from God, not something you have to earn. Words can't express the joy I felt when I read those words."

Mary is one of thousands of former Jehovah's Witnesses who have escaped from the organization. Some have left because they could no longer live with the inconsistencies of Society policy and teaching, but they have found no replacement for their belief system. Others, like Mary, have found a relationship with Jesus Christ that frees them from the bondage they experienced as Witnesses.

The Watch Tower organization is now over one hundred years old and appears destined to complete the twentieth century in more or less its present form. It has sustained itself through a century of false prophecies and generations of Jehovah's Witnesses, all of whom have bought the story that the end of the world is just around the corner and they will never have to die. Millions of persons have handed their lives over to a group of men and an organization that they accept as, and call, the "truth." They are convinced that the Watch Tower Society's leadership is the "faithful and discreet slave" used by God, and that all other religions are false.

Many Witnesses will remain in the organization all their lives. Many others will be disfellowshipped for a variety of reasons. And many more will leave the organization on their own, disillusioned by what they discover about the history and record of the Watch Tower. A few will remain in the organization and strive for reform, unaware that individually they will have no effect. The power is in the hands of a few at the upper levels, and these persons are interested only in unity at all costs—a unity that is in reality conformity.

For those who do leave, the process is usually painful. Ollie Mork wrote to us to share the pain of a separated family after he left the organization. "Now we are starting our retirement years and find we have completely lost two of our three children. Our youngest daughter recently had our second grandson, but both that fact and her wedding were kept secret from us, even though she lives nearby. My wife has not had a word from this ardent pioneer for over five years."

Gaila Noble was an active Witness for 20 years before "the scales fell from my eyes." But leaving was a traumatic experience. "I knew that the Watchtower Society had lied to me," she told us. "But the irony is that the emotions didn't follow suit. The emotions are still captive. I left Jehovah's Witnesses only to suffer as I never suffered before, mainly because I isolated myself. I was fearful—fearful of the Witnesses because I knew there was something wrong with them, fearful of the churches because my old teachings were still ingrained, fearful of my neighbors, even fearful of myself and my own thoughts. I didn't know if the devil was deceiving me or God was punishing me. I was suicidal for eight months. Finding out that your religion is a fake is much like finding out that one's own mother is a hooker."

However painful the leaving, it is still better than living in the lie. Gaila began to recover from her depression when she realized that her emotions were connected to her mind. When she changed her thinking, her feelings followed. She began thinking about Bible promises such as these words of Christ: "Where two or more are gathered in my name, there I am also," and "Come unto me, all you who are heavy laden, and I will give you rest." Jehovah's Witnesses have the right to *believe* but not to *deceive*. Nevertheless, they will continue to proselytize, not disclosing to the convert exactly what they are getting into. The Watch Tower organization will become even more intolerant of dissent and even more authoritarian in form. Although the organization fought and won many court battles over the issue of freedom of speech and religion in the 1930's and 1940's, it has removed these rights from its own adherents. Interestingly, the following quotation was printed in the September 8, 1979, issue of *Awake!* on page 7:

> It often happened that whenever a certain group obtained certain rights, they afterward had little regard for the rights of others.

The following lofty words were printed in the May 1, 1976, *Watchtower*, on page 259:

> Humans have a natural desire for freedom. They want to speak their beliefs freely without being muzzled or persecuted, and to worship according to their conscience.

However, the fact of the matter is that millions of Witnesses must conform to the party line. They are not allowed to let their Bible-trained conscience lead them in religious doctrine, beliefs, and application. They must accept whatever the leadership dictates, under threat of disfellowshipment for any deviation or freedom of expression. The July 8, 1972, *Watchtower*, on page 9, stated:

> A real test of how secure guarantees of freedom are is to try to exercise them where your viewpoint is in conflict with that of the majority or of those in power.

The deceitful Watch Tower leadership will attempt to stretch and defend their chronology. We won't be surprised if they fabricate a persecution or call the current dissidence by former Witnesses "persecution" in order to bolster enthusiasm among their members. It has been observed that when a religious movement is losing steam and when all other efforts to maintain enthusiasm prove futile, the claim of persecution never fails to rally the faithful. Persecution contains the pure ring of rightness in the fanatic's mind.

The authoritarian regimentation of Jehovah's Witnesses by their leadership will increase because that is the only way the leaders can hold the organization together. At the large district conventions of Jehovah's Witnesses held in 1987, Witnesses were counseled that they should consider the wisdom of staying single, or if married, the wisdom of not having children, because the end is so near. They were also cajoled concerning their laxity in door-to-door work. They were reminded that the Society needs more contributions for expansion. They were once again instructed that the taking of a blood transfusion breaks God's law. They were corrected for their lack of appreciation of what Jehovah was doing for them through His organization. In other words, the message hasn't changed.

Watchtower leadership is content only when total control of the membership is under the "theocratic" government. Although Witnesses may be found throughout the world and are therefore citizens of various countries, they are first and foremost citizens of the Brooklyn "theocracy." They are slaves to the masters of deception in Brooklyn and continue to be victimized by them.

In the January 22, 1964, *Awake!* on page 15, an article quoted the late Supreme Court Justice Brandeis:

Once people of supposed superior intelligence begin to impose their will on other citizens because they feel they must do their thinking for them, then society is no longer a free state, but is in a slave state.

Jehovah's Witnesses have given over their free will and thinking to the will of the organization as interpreted by the Governing Body.

Recent court cases have affirmed that the First Amendment guarantee of freedom of religion will continue to protect the Watch Tower organization in the years ahead. In other words, it has permission to run roughshod over its members, disfellowshipping and shunning them, splitting families, and causing mental breakdowns and suicide.

Nevertheless, there is hope for the lost.

Setting the Prisoners Free

At no other time in Watch Tower history has there been such a steady flow of defections from the movement. And this has provided a great field of opportunity for Christians to share their personal testimony and witness. The field is white for harvest among Jehovah's Witnesses. Many are disillusioned with the authoritarian works program they find themselves in. The numerous false prophecies and doctrinal vacillations are indefensible. The split-up of families and divorces due to Watch Tower rules and regulations are mounting. Witnesses are becoming increasingly aware that they are being held hostage in their "spiritual paradise" by the leaders. Many are wondering, "If this is such a spiritual paradise, then why am I so unhappy?" They ask, "If this is such a spiritual paradise, how come we are instructed to report on each other? How come our shepherds, the elders, are more like policemen?"

During the past ten years approximately one million persons have left the movement, either voluntarily or by disfellowshipment. We expect the exodus to continue in the years ahead, which presents an interesting challenge.

Christians have the opportunity to reach out in love to Jehovah's Witnesses. True, it is necessary to be prepared, so as not to become entangled in their web. But when a Witness knocks on our door, we can plant a seed of doubt or perhaps water what someone else has planted. Thousands of Witnesses have left the Watch Tower and become Christians in the truest sense. We can find them in various churches and fellowships throughout the world.

Many of these people have started outreach ministries to their former brothers and sisters still in the Watch Tower system. There are literally hundreds of such ministries around the world. They have joined the ranks of numerous outreach ministries run by Christians who were never Jehovah's Witnesses and who have been engaged in this work for many years.

The greatest enemy of the Watch Tower organization is its own literature. Many of the outreach groups have produced excellent material and documentation to show the error of the Watch Tower. The Society has printed itself into a corner, and these groups point out the cover-ups and false prophecies. More important, the counterarguments are Bible-based and do not rely on the fabrications and fantasies of a small group of men for authority.

We the authors saw a need to help our former brothers and sisters who are struggling to break free from the spiritual bondage of the Watch Tower system. We also felt a need to warn and inform Christians and other persons of the threat of the Watch Tower Society. To that end we formed an outreach ministry— Good News Defenders—which provides accurate information, including lecture tapes, videos, publications, and documentation. In 1987 we completed production of the film *Witnesses of Jehovah*, which was coproduced with Jeremiah Films.

Many readers will be distressed by what we have written. To those persons we humbly state, "Have I therefore become your enemy by telling you the truth?" (Galatians 4:16). It was not our purpose in writing this book to offend individuals and hurt their feelings or sensitivities. Rather, we hope that many will be released from Watch Tower bondage, and that many more will be warned of the snare of the Watch Tower and not fall victim to it.

In the preface we quoted a Watchtower publication. We wish to do the same in conclusion. In the book *Religion*, by Judge

Rutherford, published in 1940, is the following statement on page 138 that expresses our feelings about this book:

> Let it be understood that what is here said is not directed against individuals nor prompted by hate, but against a system, the offices of which are filled by men, and it is the religion and religious system that have brought great reproach upon Jehovah's name, and such fraud he now exposes by his Word of truth.

Notes

Chapter 1—A History of Disappointments

1. *The Watchtower*, September 1, 1985, p. 22.

Chapter 2—Snake-Oil Religion

1. *The Watchtower*, W.T.B.T.S., January 1, 1955, p. 7.
2. *The Finished Mystery*, W.T.B.T.S., 1917, p. 53.
3. Jonsson, *The Gentile Times Reconsidered* (Hart Publishers, 1983), Ch. 1.
4. Ibid., pp. 38-39.
5. *Zion's Watch Tower*, W.T.B.T.S., reprints, p. 3822.
6. Ibid., p. 214.
7. Ibid., p. 241.
8. Gruss, *Apostles of Denial* (Presbyterian & Reformed Pub. Co., 1970), p. 43.
9. *Zion's Watch Tower*, W.T.B.T.S., reprints, p. 224.
10. Ibid., p. 225.
11. *The Watch Tower*, W.T.B.T.S., reprints, p. 4790.
12. Gardner, *Fads and Fallacies in the Name of Science* (New York: Dover Publications, 1957), p. 174.
13. *Watchtower Cost List*, W.T.B.T.S., February 1, 1944.
14. *The Finished Mystery*, W.T.B.T.S., 1917, pp. 386-87.
15. Ibid., p. 387.
16. Ibid.
17. *The Watch Tower*, W.T.B.T.S., reprints, p. 4685.
18. Ibid.
19. Ibid., p. 1355.
20. *Studies in the Scriptures*, Vol. II, W.T.B.T.S., p. 101.
21. Ibid., p. 245.
22. *The Watch Tower*, W.T.B.T.S., reprints, pp. 5268, 5689, 5691.
23. Ibid., p. 6009.

Chapter 3—Advertise the King and His Kingdom

1. *Light after Darkness* (privately published 23-page booklet), September 1, 1917.
2. Penton, *Apocalypse Delayed* (University of Toronto Press, 1985), pp. 49-54.
3. Harrison, *Visions of Glory* (New York: Simon and Schuster, 1978), p. 170.
4. *Holy Spirit—The Force Behind the Coming New Order*, W.T.B.T.S., 1976, pp. 145-46.
5. *Millions Now Living Will Never Die*, W.T.B.T.S., 1920, p. 88.
6. Ibid., p. 97.
7. *Jehovah's Witnesses in the Divine Purpose*, W.T.B.T.S., 1959, p. 102.
8. Ibid.
9. Penton, *Apocalypse Delayed*, p. 61, graph.
10. *Yearbook*, W.T.B.T.S., 1975, p. 146.
11. Baumann, *Kensington-Talmadge 1910-1985* (self-published, 1984), p. 73.
12. Grant deed recorded February 7, 1930.
13. Ibid.
14. Franz, *Crisis of Conscience* (Atlanta: Commentary Press, 1983), p. 24.
15. *Prohibition and The League of Nations*, W.T.B.T.S., 1930, p. 36.
16. W. F. Salter letter dated April 1, 1937.
17. *The Watchtower*, W.T.B.T.S., December 1, 1987, p. 20.
18. Harrison, *Visions of Glory*, 1978, p. 74.
19. Penton, *Apocalypse Delayed*, 1985, p. 72.
20. Ibid., pp. 266, 356.
21. *Salvation*, W.T.B.T.S., 1939, p. 311.

Chapter 4—The Watchtower Theocracy

1. *Life Everlasting in Freedom of the Sons of God*, W.T.B.T.S., 1966, pp. 31-35.
2. *Yearbook*, W.T.B.T.S., 1975, p. 30.
3. *Yearbook*, W.T.B.T.S., 1976, p. 30.
4. *The Watchtower*, May 1, 1967, p. 262.

5. *Kingdom Ministry*, W.T.B.T.S., March 1968.
6. *The Watchtower*, May 1, 1968, p. 272.
7. *Jehovah's Witnesses in the Divine Purpose*, W.T.B.T.S., 1959, pp. 148-49.
8. *Yearbook*, W.T.B.T.S., 1975, p. 88.
9. *God's Kingdom of a Thousand Years Has Approached*, W.T.B.T.S., 1973, pp. 345-46.
10. *The Divine Plan of the Ages*, W.T.B.T.S., 1927 edition, p. 7.
11. *Jehovah's Witnesses in the Divine Purpose*, W.T.B.T.S., 1959, p. 95.
12. *The Watch Tower*, reprints, W.T.B.T.S., p. 6159.
13. *The Watchtower*, December 15, 1977, pp. 750-51.
14. *The Watchtower*, October 15, 1966, p. 623.

Chapter 5—Finding True Freedom in Jesus Christ

1. *The Watchtower*, May 15, 1969, p. 312.
2. *Kingdom Ministry*, W.T.B.T.S., May 1974.
3. *Awake!* W.T.B.T.S., November 8, 1974, p. 11.
4. *The Watchtower*, July 15, 1976, pp. 440-41.

Chapter 6—Chronological Deception

1. Jonsson, *The Gentile Times Reconsidered*, p. 4.
2. Ibid., p. 5.
3. Ibid., p. v.
4. *Spectrum*, Vol. II, No. 4, 1981, p. 63. (Noted in *The Gentile Times Reconsidered*, p. 6.)
5. Jonsson, *The Gentile Times Reconsidered*, p. 140.
6. Franz, *Crisis of Conscience*, pp. 25-26.
7. Jonsson, *The Gentile Times Reconsidered*, pp. 146-47.
8. *Awake!* September 22, 1962, p. 27.
9. *The Watchtower*, June 1, 1966, p. 326.
10. *Awake!* October 8, 1966, pp. 18-19.
11. *Awake!* October 8, 1968, pp. 13-14.
12. *Awake!* October 8, 1971, p. 26.
13. *The Watchtower*, October 1, 1978, p. 31.

14. *The Watchtower*, October 15, 1980, p. 31.
15. Ibid.
16. Franz, *Crisis of Conscience*, pp. 218-20.

Chapter 7—Big Mother

1. *The Watchtower*, February 1, 1952, p. 80.
2. Ibid., p. 79.
3. Ibid., p. 80.
4. *The Watchtower*, May 1, 1957, p. 274.
5. Ibid.
6. Ibid.
7. Ibid., p. 284.
8. *The Watchtower*, June 15, 1957, p. 370.
9. *The Watchtower*, May 1, 1961, p. 274.
10. *The Watchtower*, October 1, 1967, p. 587.
11. Flo Conway & Jim Siegelman, *Snapping* (Dell Publishing Co., 1978), p. 170.
12. *The Watchtower*, January 15, 1983, p. 22.
13. Ibid., p. 27.
14. *The Watchtower*, February 15, 1976, p. 124.
15. *The Watchtower*, December 1, 1981, p. 27.
16. *The Watchtower*, December 15, 1983, p. 30.
17. *The Watchtower*, May 1, 1984, p. 31.

Chapter 8—Jehovah's Happy Organization

1. George Orwell, *1984* (Harcourt Brace Jovanovich, Inc., 1949), p. 32.
2. Ibid., p. 205.
3. *The Watchtower*, March 1, 1979, pp. 23-24.
4. *The Watch Tower*, reprints, March 1, 1915, p. 5649.
5. *Light*, W.T.B.T.S., Vol. 1, 1930, p. 194.
6. *The Watchtower*, September 1, 1985, p. 24.
7. Orwell, *1984*, p. 176.
8. Ibid.
9. Ibid., p. 64.
10. Ibid., p. 37.

11. *The Watchtower*, November 15, 1985, p. 21.

12. Ibid., p. 19.

13. Botting, *The Orwellian World of Jehovah's Witnesses* (University of Toronto Press, 1984), p. XIX.

14. Orwell, *1984*, p. 220.

15. From a personal letter.

16. Orwell, *1984*, p. 173.

17. Ibid., p. 19.

18. Ibid., p. 221.

19. Gruss, *We Left Jehovah's Witnesses—A Non-Prophet Organization* (Presbyterian and Reformed Publishing Co., 1974), p. 95.

20. Orwell, *1984*, p. 54.

21. Ibid., p. 70.

22. Ibid., p. 220.

23. Ibid., p. 175.

24. Ibid., p. 69.

Chapter 9—A Different Gospel

1. *The Watchtower*, May 1, 1981, p. 17.

2. *The Watchtower*, October 1, 1980, p. 28.

3. *The Truth that leads to Eternal Life*, W.T.B.T.S., 1968, p. 82.

4. Ibid., pp. 102-03.

5. Ibid.

6. Ibid., p. 104.

7. Reed, *Jehovah's Witnesses Answered Verse by Verse* (Baker Book House, 1986), p. 107.

8. *The Truth that leads to Eternal Life*, pp. 104-05.

9. *Man's Salvation Out of World Distress at Hand!* W.T.B.T.S., 1975, pp. 361-63.

10. *The Truth that leads to Eternal Life*, pp. 106-07.

11. Ibid., pp. 112-13.

12. Ibid., pp. 94-95.

13. *Organized to Accomplish Our Ministry*, W.T.B.T.S., 1983, pp. 92-93.

14. *The Watchtower*, November 15, 1976, pp. 686-87.

15. Ibid., p. 689.

Chapter 10—Savior Angel

1. *Then Is Finished The Mystery of God*, W.T.B.T.S., 1969, pp. 249, 306-07.
2. *You Can Live Forever In Paradise On Earth*, W.T.B.T.S., 1982, p. 58.
3. Ibid.
4. *Barnes' Notes on the New Testament* (Grand Rapids: Kregel Publications), p. 1099.
5. *The Watchtower*, April 15, 1956, pp. 238-39.
6. *Life Everlasting in Freedom of the Sons of God*, p. 75.
7. *You Can Live Forever In Paradise On Earth*, p. 62.
8. *The Watchtower*, September 1, 1953, p. 517.
9. Ibid., p. 518.
10. *Zion's Watch Tower*, February 1888, reprints, p. 1005.
11. *My Book of Bible Stories*, W.T.B.T.S., 1978, p. 102.
12. *Awake!* September 22, 1976, p. 27.
13. *Your Will Be Done On Earth*, W.T.B.T.S., 1958, p. 316.
14. *The Watchtower*, September 15, 1961, p. 552.
15. *The Watchtower*, April 15, 1956, p. 237.
16. *The Watchtower*, November 15, 1979, p. 26.
17. *The Watchtower*, December 1, 1985, p. 17.
18. *The Watchtower*, February 15, 1986, p. 20.

Chapter 11—The Occult Connection

1. *Zion's Watch Tower*, October 1907, reprints, p. 4069.
2. Johannes Greber was used as a biblical authority in the following publications:

   The Watchtower, September 15, 1962, p. 554.
   The Watchtower, October 15, 1975, p. 640.
   The Watchtower, April 15, 1976, p. 231.
   "The Word"—Who Is He? According To John, W.T.B.T.S., 1962, p. 5.
   Make Sure Of All Things; Hold Fast To What Is Fine, W.T.B.T.S. (1965 edition), p. 489.
   Aid to Bible Understanding, W.T.B.T.S., 1969, 1971, p. 1134.
   Ibid., p. 1669.

Chapter 12—Life-and-Death Choices

1. Gardner, *Fads and Fallacies in the Name of Science*, p. 206.
2. *The Golden Age*, W.T.B.T.S., May 1, 1929, p. 502.
3. *The Golden Age*, January 9, 1929, p. 245.
4. Gruss, *We Left Jehovah's Witnesses*, p. 65.
5. *The Watchtower*, December 15, 1952, p. 764.
6. *Awake!* August 22, 1965, p. 20.
7. *Yearbook*, W.T.B.T.S., 1975, p. 222.
8. *The Watch Tower*, December 15, 1927, p. 371.
9. *The Watchtower*, February 15, 1939, p. 62.
10. *Awake!* October 22, 1948, p. 12.
11. *Awake!* May 22, 1951, p. 5.
12. *Awake!* February 22, 1975, p. 30.

Chapter 14—The Exodus

1. Information in this account is taken from *I Found The Truth: When I Left the Watchtower* (Columbus, Georgia: The Watchman Fellowship, Inc.).

Other Good Harvest House Reading

ANSWERS TO THE CULTIST AT YOUR DOOR
by *Robert and Gretchen Passantino*

This book is for anyone who wants a basic understanding of the cults without undue research! Concise reviews and answers to the beliefs of Jehovah's Witnesses, Hare Krishnas, The Way International, Mormons, and Moonies. Highly recommended by Walter Martin.

THE GOD MAKERS
by *Ed Decker* and *Dave Hunt*

This unique exposé on Mormonism is factual, carefully researched, and fully documented. *The God Makers* provides staggering new insights that go beyond the explosive film of the same title. An excellent tool in reaching Mormons.

THE CULT EXPLOSION
by *Dave Hunt*

This book exposes the real danger and the strategies employed by cults of our time. Must reading for anyone who wants to understand the subtle ways cults prey upon the fears and needs of so many people.

FALSE GODS OF OUR TIME
by *Norm Geisler*

Norm Geisler clarifies two major views of God that clamor for the attention of modern man. Being aware of what these are and their influence on our society is critical to dealing effectively with the 20th-century mindset and leading new believers to the Truth.

THE BEAUTIFUL SIDE OF EVIL
by *Johanna Michaelsen*

Hal Lindsey's sister-in-law shares her extraordinary story about her involvement in the occult and how she learned to distinguish between the beautiful side of evil and the true way of the Lord.

OUT ON A BROKEN LIMB
by *F. LaGard Smith*

Millions of people have been exposed to the teachings of reincarnation, Eastern mysticism, and the New Age Movement through actress Shirley MacLaine's autobiography *Out on a Limb*. F. LaGard Smith explores the biblical meaning of life and afterlife in this answer to the MacLaine book.

AMERICA: THE SORCERER'S NEW APPRENTICE
by *Dave Hunt* and *T.A. McMahon*

Many respected experts predict that America is at the threshold of a glorious New Age. Other equally notable observers warn that Eastern mysticism, at the heart of the New Age Movement, will eventually corrupt Western civilization.

The question is, *Who is right*? Is there really a threat to the American way of life as we know it? Will we be able to distinguish between the true hope of the Gospel and the false hope of the New Age?

Dave Hunt and T.A. McMahon, bestselling authors of *The Seduction of Christianity* break down the most brilliant arguments of the most-respected New Age leaders. This bold new book is an up-to-date Christian apologetic, presenting overwhelming evidence for the superiority of the Christian faith.

SATAN'S UNDERGROUND
by *Lauren Stratford*

Lauren Stratford was abused and tortured as a child, and as a young adult found herself caught in a painful web of pornography, satanism, and ritualistic abuse. Her story is a difficult one to hear. Lauren openly shares her dramatic story from personal devastation to complete liberation so that others may find healing and freedom through the love of Jesus. It is a true testimony of the power of God to take the most tragic circumstances and turn them into blessings. Foreword by Johanna Michaelsen and Hal Lindsey. Highly recommended by Mike Warnke.

Dear Reader:

We would appreciate hearing from you regarding this Harvest House nonfiction book. It will enable us to continue to give you the best in Christian publishing.

1. What most influenced you to purchase *Witnesses of Jehovah?*
   - ☐ Author
   - ☐ Subject matter
   - ☐ Backcover copy
   - ☐ Recommendations
   - ☐ Cover/Title
   - ☐ _____

2. Where did you purchase this book?
   - ☐ Christian bookstore
   - ☐ General bookstore
   - ☐ Department store
   - ☐ Grocery store
   - ☐ Other

3. Your overall rating of this book:
   - ☐ Excellent   ☐ Very good   ☐ Good   ☐ Fair   ☐ Poor

4. How likely would you be to purchase other books by this author?
   - ☐ Very likely
   - ☐ Somewhat likely
   - ☐ Not very likely
   - ☐ Not at all

5. What types of books most interest you?
   (check all that apply)
   - ☐ Women's Books
   - ☐ Marriage Books
   - ☐ Current Issues
   - ☐ Self Help/Psychology
   - ☐ Bible Studies
   - ☐ Fiction
   - ☐ Biographies
   - ☐ Children's Books
   - ☐ Youth Books
   - ☐ Other _____

6. Please check the box next to your age group.
   - ☐ Under 18
   - ☐ 18-24
   - ☐ 25-34
   - ☐ 35-44
   - ☐ 45-54
   - ☐ 55 and over

Mail to: Editorial Director
Harvest House Publishers
1075 Arrowsmith
Eugene, OR 97402

Name _____

Address _____

City _____ State _____ Zip _____

Thank you for helping us to help you in future publications!

NOW SEE THE REVEALING FILM

Contact your local Christian Film Distributor
or write to:
Malaga Cove Pictures
P.O. Box 2704
Huntington Beach, California 92647
or call:

1-800-824-1605 U.S.
1-714-840-4606 CA

For further information on Jehovah's Witnesses, or
an order form of materials available, including the
video-cassette *Witnesses of Jehovah*, contact:

Leonard Chretien, Director
Good News Defenders
P.O. Box 8007
La Jolla, California 92038